INSURANCE
RIPOFFS
AND
DIRTY TRICKS

To MARY ANN —
CHEERS ANYWAY !)

Willart

INSURANCE RIPOFFS

AND

DIRTY TRICKS

THE SUCKER'S DILEMMA

The Earth Is Flat...Pigs Can Fly And

You Can Always Trust Your Insurance Company

A Tirade And Harangue

For Policyholders, Claimants,

Agents, Brokers And All Other Victims

Harold F. Willard, A.R.P.c.

Illustrations by Gordon Anderson

THUMBSDOWNBOOKS
San Diego, California

Published by
THUMBSDOWNBOOKS
~~P.O. Box 83912, San Diego, CA 92138-3912~~
PO BX 961 KIRKLAND 98083-0961

Permission to quote excerpts from the following copyrighted
material is gratefully acknowledged:

The Health Insurance Racket and How to Beat It by John E. Gregg,
copyright © 1973.

Pay Now, Die Later by James Gollin. Copyright © 1966 by James
Gollin. Reprinted by permission of Random House, Inc.

"Greed Is Ruining Industrial Base" by Roger A. Evans, copyright ©
1985.

"The Strangest Planet of All" by Art Hoppe, copyright © 1968
Chronicle Publishing Company. Reprinted with permission of the
author.

1897 Sears Roebuck Catalogue, edited by Fred L. Israel, copyright ©
1968 by Chelsea House Publishers.

"Can We Insure Against Insurers" by William F. Buckley, copyright ©
1978.

Ready For The Plaintiff by Melvin Belli copyright © 1956.

Design by Words & Deeds, Los Angeles

Printed in the United States of America

ISBN 0-943061-04-0

ACKNOWLEDGMENTS

I am indebted to the bad vibes emanating from the private insurance industry for the impressions in this book.

I thank the authors of more than one hundred and fifty pounds of books that support the general validity of these impressions.

I wish to thank specifically the "Colossal Benefit" Insurance Company for supplying the final swindle that motivated the gathering of this material.

Public Tolerance

Rodent Damage

CONTENTS

PART I

PART II

PART III

PART IV

PREFACE

I have earned the coveted title of A.R.P.c. for being **A RATHER PIGHEADED claimant**. Pigheadedness helps to convert the insurance industry's flamboyant shams, improprieties and overt greed into something with a value.

This book is about real insurance atrocities as seen by a victim, presented in a fictional format. It is not about the benefits that find their way through the maze of fine print in policies written solely to maximize profits and flimflam the unwary.

This is a combination of poor me-ism and poor you-ism. It is not insurance counseling, it is a tirade. If cheating is suspected, consult a trial lawyer specializing in insurance bad faith.

Unprincipled insurance companies that fleece the public, then wheel and deal in the economy with the proceeds, can be compared to organized crime investing in legitimate business. It invites economic collapse.

The insurance industry cannot be called all bad. The good guys outnumber the bad guys. The hard-core bad guys may be found in top management and among the actuaries who calculate the mathematical basis for huge swindles. Bad guys exist among company attorneys who defend the ripoffs and claims adjusters with cast-iron consciences who negotiate the fine-print swindles. Lawmakers who legalize an assortment of bad-guy activities also must be included in this group.

The insurance industry could make a fair profit *without* double talk, *without* deception and *without* cheating; *without* indiscriminate claim-dodging and *without* pleading ruinous losses while stashing huge sums of loot in untaxed reserves.

Typically, insurance people will deny the validity of what they read in this book, but there is no denying the hard fact that this is the way it looks to countless victims and a number of experts.

There is no place to hide. Insurance is compulsory for nearly everyone in our country. Liability insurance is forced by law on motorists and businesses. Fire and casualty insurance is required nationwide on all mortgages and automotive financing. This windfall of captive business, added to the business amassed by high pressure sales methods, has left the insurance industry in control of more than $600 billion of our nation's wealth!

Insurance companies cast envious eyes on oil company profits generated by the oil "shortage," so they concocted a new product. It is called an "insurance shortage" with coverage decreased, deductibles increased, rates raised to unaffordable levels and less lucrative policies canceled from coast to coast. Some companies claim these actions are necessary because damage awards are too high when claimants are forced into court to collect their legitimate benefits.

It is not possible for the nation's insurance companies, all at the same time, to claim a "shortage of insurance" without some kind of collusion.

As this is being written, the California Attorney General's office is investigating 125 insurance companies to determine if the industry's activities are in violation of the state's insurance code and antitrust laws. It became necessary to use subpoena powers to compel the companies to produce documents because it was evident that they would not respond fully otherwise.

The insurance industry's disregard for the public interest has created a manufactured crisis so severe that more than two-thirds of California's cities may be forced to self-insure; daycare centers have closed; bars, churches, private schools, boy scout troops, nursery schools, roller coasters, hiking trails in wildlife areas and countless small businesses have canceled activities or gone out of business entirely. The list of victims grows daily.

Insurance principles are school-kid simple. Insurance schemes, on the other hand, have been deliberately complicated to milk every possible dollar out of gullible policyholders. Fine-print piracy and dirty dealing are rampant in the "protection rackets" and their financial booby-traps create serious problems for policyholders, claimants, even insurance personnel. When insurance buyers and job applicants overlook these shortcomings, they eventually find themselves in unforeseen and often serious trouble.

Don and Connie Easymark; Shafter, Judas & Sly; Madeline Megabucks; Jim Reilly; Mike Ross; Dr. Phastbuck; John Q. Sucker; Arnie Flugelman; the Colossal Benefit Insurance Company; Charles Alyson Chumpworth, Jr.; Matilda and Richard Potter; Jameston, Jameston, Grover & Lipinsky are all fictional characters involved in documented insurance ripoffs.

Any resemblance to actual victims or existing companies is a coincidence, although indeed a sad fact of life.

My intention is to focus attention on a few matters of interest to insurance buyers and sellers alike. If by chance I should help the reader avoid being trapped in the financial maw of some dishonest company...so be it!

WARNING — DISCLAIMER

In the following chapters, words such as thievery, fraud, trickery, deception and impropriety are clearly based on my long-standing opinion that insurance cheating has exploded into a massive scheme to make money without honoring the obligation to protect the interests of policyholders and casualty victims.

Although most insurance activities are legal under current law, I strongly disagree with the fairness of the business methods and tactics of *renegade* companies.

This is purely a layman's view of fictional people burdened with real-world insurance ripoffs. The purpose of this book is to entertain and to trigger caution.

THIS IS NOT LEGAL ADVICE.

If dishonesty is suspected, consult a trial lawyer specializing in insurance problems.

I'M ONLY THE BOOKKEEPER
(You Easymark!)

It is easier to eat a Chinese dinner with one chopstick than to escape the scourge of insurance ripoffs and dirty tricks.

If you feel an urge to talk about people who have been overcharged, underpaid, flimflammed or fine-printed, you will have a problem: a problem deciding where to begin. Betty Jameston is probably as good a beginning as any.

"I wouldn't know, I'm only the bookkeeper. That's up to Mr. Shafter; he employs me and I follow his orders."

It was Betty's first day with the Shafter, Judas & Sly Insurance Agency. She had never expected to work for such a colorful trio of "financial advisers": Mr. Shafter, meticulously groomed, with a quick, deceptively sincere smile; Tom Judas, with sharp, thin features and a nervous tic giving the impression of a friendly wink; Sam Sly, pudgy and white-faced, with a roadmap of broken blood vessels on his cheeks and folds of fat on his neck draping over his starched collar.

Attractive, twenty-three-year-old Betty had been under-classified as a clerical trainee to justify the low pay of insurance clerks. Her father was senior partner in Jameston, Jameston, Grover & Lipinsky, a firm of trial lawyers. Betty had her father's alert and analytical mind.

Sam Sly said policyholders were easymarks. He instructed Betty to reply to hostile clients by saying, "I wouldn't know, I'm only the bookkeeper. That's up to Mr. Shafter."

5

She wondered why clients should be hostile and why such evasive language should be necessary. Before the day was over, she no longer wondered why such language was necessary.

"The mere fact that you found your window open and your TV missing doesn't mean there was a burglary. There are no tool marks, broken locks or windows, so we must respectfully deny your claim."

MADELINE MEGABUCKS

Betty sat alone behind the counter nervously trying to decide how she would answer clients' questions about insurance. The brokers were out of the office, doing whatever brokers do when they are out of the office. Betty's prior dealings with insurance consisted mainly of sending money when premium notices arrived in the mail. She was unsure of herself on the receiving end of the insurance money game.

Her preoccupation was interrupted by the arrival of an expensively dressed, middle-aged woman. The angry clicking of her high heels on the floor sounded ominous as she approached the counter.

"Young lady, I want to speak to Mr. Sly, and I want to speak to him now!"

"I'm sorry, Ma'am, Mr. Sly is out of the office. Who shall I say called?"

"I am Madeline Megabucks, and I want you to report to Mr. Sly that my two-and-a-half-carat, emerald-cut diamond ring was among the items stolen in a burglary the night before last. I was led to believe it was covered by my homeowners policy. The Colossal Benefit claims office tells me jewelry taken in a burglary is among the exclusions in my policy. I tried to read the policy, but most of it seemed to be legalistic gibberish. It appears, however, that my ring would have been fully covered if it had been blown away by the wind or struck by lightning! What am I going to do?"

"I'm sorry, Mrs. Megabucks, I can't advise you; I'm only the bookkeeper. I'll report this to Mr. Sly when he returns."

Betty Jameston was beginning to understand the value of saying, "I'm only the bookkeeper," and leaving the complaints for the professionals to answer. Her thoughts were interrupted by the office door swinging open. A clean-cut young construction worker wearing a hard hat stormed in and slammed his lunchbox down on the counter.

JIM REILLY

"Where's that con artist, Tom Judas? I want to talk to him and I mean right now!"

"I'm sorry, sir, Mr. Judas is out of the office. May I give

him a message or tell him who called?"

"My name is Jim Reilly. That flannel-mouthed Judas told me my homeowners policy protected everything. Last night's windstorm brought down the big beautiful Blue Spruce tree in my front yard and blew in the leaded glass window in my den. The bony-assed old witch in the Colossal Benefit claims office politely refused to pay for either one of them. According to the fine print in my policy, the tree would have been fully covered if it had *exploded* and the window would have been covered only if it had blown *outward* instead of inward! Just what the hell am I supposed to do now?"

"I really wouldn't know, Mr. Reilly. I'm only the book-keeper. I'll report what you said to Mr. Judas when he returns."

CAPTAIN ROSS

Several days passed before Betty was again faced with an explosive reaction to the sales tactics and business methods of the Colossal Benefit Insurance Company.

She was, as usual, alone in the office. She answered the persistent ring of the telephone with, "Thank you for calling Shafter, Judas & Sly. May I help you?"

A woman's voice said, "Oh, please Ma'am, do be careful. My husband, Captain Ross, is headed for your office with a complaint. Don't argue with him; he's a very violent man... Oh my goodness I must hang up now; here he comes back. He must have forgotten his car keys." CLICK.

Betty sat back and waited. She questioned the adequacy of an insurance clerk's salary. She shuddered and she waited. She wished the brokers were in the office. Even Sam Sly would have been welcome. She shuffled papers and she waited.

The office door swung open silently and a huge man with a bulge under his coat loomed up at the counter, his hard blue eyes taking in every detail of the office. Betty remained at her desk.

"May I help you, sir?"

"Who's in charge of this automated policy mill?"

"That would be Mr. Shafter."

"Well, get off your duff, little lady, and get him out here fast."

"I'm sorry sir, he's out of the office. May I take a message for him?"

"Yes, you may, but you listen, little lady, and you listen good, because I'm only going to say this once! I'm Captain Mike Ross of the Center City Bunko Squad. I just discovered that my 78-year-old mother and my 82-year-old father have delayed repairing their refrigerator, television and stove because they were trying to keep up with $2,882 in yearly premiums on nineteen insurance policies that they need like they need three airplanes! Seventeen of those nineteen policies have your stamp on them. Pay attention now, because I'm giving you exactly five days to cancel those policies and return their money or we'll immediately take other measures! Goodbye, little lady."

He left as silently as he had arrived.

MATILDA POTTER

Several days passed without excessive stress. All was quiet in the office. Maybe this wasn't going to be such a bad job after all. Without unwelcome interruptions, Betty kept busy with routine office work and learning the intricacies of the agency's new word processor.

Betty was once again alone in the office. The brokers and agents were attending a sales psychology seminar that included a chicken à la king luncheon at the Tahitian Paradise Motel and Convention Center.

In a little room at the rear of the Shafter, Judas & Sly insurance office, there was always a ten-ounce, yellow-labeled jar of generic instant coffee and a pot of hot water supplied courtesy of the management. Betty went to the back room for a cup of coffee.

When she returned to the front office, a woman dressed in black was waiting quietly at the counter.

"May I help you, Ma'am?"

The woman appeared to be in shock. She stared blankly at Mr. Shafter's locked office door. "I must talk to the Colossal Benefit broker, please."

"I'm sorry, he is attending a seminar today. May I tell him who called or give him a message?"

"My name is Matilda Potter. My husband, Professor Richard Potter from State College, was killed while on a personal visit to Washington, D.C. When he began work at the college he was told that one of his fringe benefits was $75,000 in Colossal Benefit group life insurance. We were given a brochure from your office saying the master policy was on file with the college and we were welcome to read it at any time. We were not very good at reading insurance policies because of the incomprehensible language. We trusted the Colossal Benefit Insurance Company because of the College's implied approval. Now they are refusing to pay the claim because Richard didn't die while working. Is there anything Mr. Shafter can do to help me?"

"I wouldn't know, Mrs. Potter, I'm only the bookkeeper. I certainly will report this to Mr. Shafter as soon as he returns."

Under her breath Betty said, "Damn it! If Mr. Shafter doesn't help, I know someone who can and will!"

Ten days later, Betty Jameston was at her desk behind the counter sealing envelopes for a direct mail pitch about the new "Cradle to Grave Financial Service" being offered by the Colossal Benefit Insurance Company.

Sam Sly and Tom Judas were opening the morning mail in the walnut-paneled office marked "Private." Sam Sly opened an envelope labeled "Urgent" from the legal department at the Colossal Benefit home office. As he read the letter, his jowls turned from oyster white to livid red. He stood up and bellowed, "Miss Jameston! Report to this office immediately! Stop whatever you're doing and get in here right now!"

Betty reported to the private office with apprehension. She stood rigid for a seemingly endless length of time under Sam Sly's cold, penetrating stare.

Finally, he spoke. "Miss Jameston, according to this letter from the home office, we're being named as co-defendants in four separate lawsuits asking for punitive damages totaling over three million dollars! They were filed by Jameston, Jameston, Grover & Lipinsky on behalf of Madeline Megabucks, Jim Reilly, Captain Ross's parents and Matilda Potter. They are alleging everything from bad faith and fraud to mopery on the king's highway! Now exactly what the hell is going on around here? Just what is bugging these people anyway?"

"I wouldn't know, Mr. Sly. I'm only the bookkeeper. You'll have to ask Mr. Shafter about that."

"I don't know when we can process your claim, sir...
our computer is down."

CLAIM DENIED
(The Bottom Line)

Donald T. Easymark, a hard working, congenial and friendly person, suffered a serious spinal injury on his job with the real estate department of the Big Shaft Oil Company. The Colossal Benefit Insurance Company stamped "Claim Denied" on his long and complicated health insurance claim form.

While Donald T. lay at home in homemade traction, the Colossal Benefit Insurance Company's investment department searched for investments paying the highest possible return on millions of dollars lying idle in its untaxed reserve fund.

The "bottom line" is the *only* thing of interest to victims of an insurance industry that grasps for colossal profit, no matter what.

"Claim Denied" was the bottom line for Donald.

Don Easymark and his wife Connie lived in a newer home in an agricultural town in the center of the vast territory he covered in his job in the state of Washington.

Don was the type who would return overpayments of change with a flourish, then note with interest the cashier's amazement.

He had been known to buy a hamburger for an emaciated stray dog when his finances were painfully low. His attitude, however, was less charitable toward fast-buck specialists in the insurance industry.

13

He was not as easy a mark as his name might imply. He had an aversion to earning money in a manner harmful to other people and reacted in a highly negative manner toward those who did.

Great wealth was not his primary goal in life. His sympathy was with the underdog and, thanks mainly to his "colossal benefits," he was to become a temporary underdog himself.

The local mini-hospital had refused to admit him because his health insurance was worthless and he was unable to afford sky-high hospital costs.

Doctor Phastbuck (the town doctor who owned a piece of the mini-hospital) suggested that he either pay for treatment in advance or go home and jury-rig traction with anything available. Bricks maybe.

Discouraged, Don limped the four long blocks from the doctor's office to his home. Each step triggered mega-volt shocks from his injured spine. Muscle spasms had wrenched his tall body out of alignment. He inched up the steps to his front door.

Always compassionate, Connie helped him into bed. Dr. Phastbuck had recommended spinal traction beginning at the hips instead of the ankles, so one of Mrs. Easymark's girdles was fitted firmly into position. This space-age miracle of modern medicine was attached by two yellow nylon cords running through pulleys to a red saddle-leather overnight bag containing the medically prescribed weight of bricks. Don had an agonized look on his face. Damaged spinal nerves cause excruciating pain. His suffering was severe.

"What in hell have I ever done to deserve this?" he moaned.

"Apparently you made the mistake of relying on a crooked insurance company for health care protection," Connie replied.

"Damnit! How am I supposed to know who's crooked and who isn't? They all act like mother hens until it's time to pay a claim, then they become the enemy!"

Connie Easymark had always felt that she would rather live in the Province of British Columbia, where *all* citizens enjoy high quality comprehensive health care through the Provincial health care system. "Don ought to have the same protection," she reasoned. "Unlike the United States, Canadian lawmakers give priority to proper health care for their citizens instead of pandering to profiteers."

The Colossal Benefit Insurance company collected the premiums, then unloaded the obligation for Don's medical bills on the taxpayers — an act possible only because of legislative stupidity, outright dishonesty, or both. In British Columbia health care is a right, like national defense and

"Mr. Easymark, Dr. Phastbuck says to put two more bricks in the bag and don't hesitate to call us any time you get any money."

police or fire protection, and is not based on the citizen's ability to pay. The quality of health care in British Columbia is as good or better than any in the world and is supplied *without routing billions of health care dollars through renegade insurance companies*. The United States is the only large industrial nation in the world that doesn't have a national health care program.

Knowing the limitations of disabled claimants, the Colossal Benefit claims department simply stonewalled on Donald Easymark's claim, forcing him to seek long overdue medical care in a Veterans Administration hospital. Too weakened to face the quagmire of insurance litigation, Don let the statute of limitations run out, thereby eliminating any hope of help through the courts.

When he recovered enough to work, he vowed to help people avoid the often long-term hardship and suffering caused by claim-dodging companies.

Don considered volunteering as an unpaid ambulance chaser and was surprised to discover that the need was non-existent. Attorneys with the necessary knowledge of insurance ripoffs were so busy they had no need for such a service, and referrals to unqualified lawyers would only make matters worse.

Donald T. Easymark made a decision. "This may be like attacking a battleship with paperclips and a rubber band, but I'm damn well going to do it anyway! I'm going to break all the rules of the claims game!"

PROBLEM CLAIMANT

Donald T. Easymark was red flagged as a "problem claimant" in the Colossal Benefit Insurance Company's computers.

Conversely, the Colossal Benefit Insurance Company was labeled a "problem company" by Donald T.

He had little to lose by defying the industry's self-serving claim system.

He began by founding a nonprofit consumer organization called G.R.I.M. (Group Resisting Insurance Misrepresentation). G.R.I.M. became known from Hawaii to the East Coast, but it was a cry in the wilderness and ineffective against the approximate 2,000 insurance companies that collected billions of dollars annually while returning as little of it as possible.

Don stopped trying to get answers from his smiling, hand-pumping, back-slapping insurance agent.

He also quit trying to get help from the understaffed, underfunded State Insurance Commissioner, who couldn't begin to protect the interests of the more than 20,000 insurance victims requesting help annually.

He stopped writing to his congressman because the only responses were form letters signed by a machine thanking him for his "views."

He decided to write a book about the negative aspects of insurance as seen through the eyes of Donald Easymark.

Although not a professional writer, he was fully capable of expressing his views in language understandable to everyone from the street sweeper in Kansas City to the professors of finance at the University of Pennsylvania's Wharton School of Business.

Don knew such a book would be a challenge. Nonetheless, focusing attention on past and present insurance atrocities had overpowering appeal. He would write about industry shortcomings as they appear to the Easymarks and let the insurance propaganda sharks brag about the benefits.

Criticism of smug, self-righteous insurers always triggers a diversionary debate, backed by a landslide of unverifiable numbers and statistics supplied by member companies and often based on something other than the particular swindle being discussed.

Debates are for experts only. Donald T. felt no desire and certainly no obligation to become such an expert. He was interested only in the problems as seen by victims.

People with professional knowledge of insurance shell games seldom were anxious to share that information with any easymark who happened to walk in off the street.

His darkest suspicions were confirmed, however, by material readily available in bookstores, newspaper files, public and university libraries and reports on congressional and Federal Trade Commission investigations.

The documented horror story that surfaced was shocking. It involved not only the health insurance rackets, but the entire industry. He found a self-righteous industry riddled with greed, dishonesty and corruption.

Separating the facts from the breastbeating and claptrappery in insurance publications was a major problem.

He learned that honest people within the industry had been duped along with policyholders and claimants. Countless agents had been "fine printed" as ruthlessly as their customers. Fine print was the backbone of the industry's pursuit of profit, regardless of the hardship to its victims.

The increasing popularity of "junk mail" marketing meant that more and more agents were being terminated for no valid cause whatever, and the renewal commissions they had worked for years to build had been cut off.

To fight this swindle, the terminated agent had to engage in expensive litigation lasting many months. The companies knew the odds and relied on the agent being starved into settling for a pittance.

Honest people within the industry have discovered too late that their chosen profession is not what it was represented to be when they filled out the job application.

Victims from outside the industry have discovered too late that their insurance company is not the guardian angel described in double-page advertisements in the weekly news magazines, T.V. commercials and junk mail.

Donald T.'s problem was in knowing where to stop writing. He had to avoid being submerged in the sea of atrocities documented in the muddy annals of the industry and in the records of the nation's courts, already overburdened with litigation traceable to insurance mischief.

FLITCRAFT
(It Must Mean *Something!*)

Donald T. tried to improve his understanding of the insurance rackets by reading insurance publications. One such publication was the 1980 edition of *Best's Flitcraft Compend*, a 928-page life insurance rate book containing more than half a million numbers all in precise little columns. Buried somewhere in those half a million numbers was the best buy for your life insurance dollar.

"Connie," he asked, "what the hell does 'Flitcraft' mean anyway? It isn't in any dictionary. Evidently, there is no such word as 'Flitcraft.' I think it's an alternative language called 'insurancese.'

"The *Oxford Dictionary* defines 'compend' as: 'A shortcut; an abridgment of a larger work.' All this stuff must be a shortcut or an abridgment of something larger!"

"That sounds truly cosmic," said Connie.

"Best's says this is the industry's most widely circulated comparative rate book, expanded to reflect many of the sales and marketing innovations of this dynamic and changing industry."

"Stupendous! A 'Best' seller, I presume."

"*Best's Flitcraft Compend* is a source of life insurance information. The policy analyses and actuarial clutter are enough to leave insurance buyers in an irreversible state of confusion and bore the socks off them as a surprise fringe benefit."

"Amen! Is that the end of your tirade?"

"No, it isn't. I'm not through yet. Let me tell you a horror story about two major types of companies that force-feed 'protection' to the nation's easymarks. It'll make your eyes water and your nose run!"

SEVERE PUNISHMENT

Don turned to Connie. "There are two basic types of companies that bully people into paying for 'protection' and both of them punish us all severely."

Connie was painting her nails. She looked up and asked, "Only two?"

"Isn't that enough?"

"What are they?" Connie screwed the cap back on the nail polish bottle.

"'Stock' and 'mutual' companies. We own two books by experts explaining the shocking details and both are right here on the den bookshelf."

"Which is easiest to understand?"

Don removed a book from the shelf. "This one by Richard Shulman, *The Billion Dollar Bookies*. It's a tough exposé of the mutual companies. Shulman is a University of California law school graduate and one of only two California state-licensed insurance analysts. It tells how mutual policyholders have been taken for hundreds of millions of dollars over the years."

Critically surveying her manicure she asked, "How were they taken?"

"A number of ways. One example is management buying back all the corporate stock, mostly with the company's own assets. This gets rid of the pesky shareholders and eliminates the annoying obligation to account to them for what is done

"... so we use company assets to buy back all the COLOSSAL
BENEFIT stock, tell the policyholders they own the company
and rename it MALARKEY MUTUAL."

with millions, and maybe billions of policyholder dollars. Management then says to the policyholders, 'We are now a mutual and you own the company, you lucky people!' which, of course, is unadulterated tripe of the worst kind!"

Not being one to leave a tirade unfinished, Don continued. "It's essentially impossible for policyholders to control the scheming in company boardrooms and totally impossible for the policyholder to sell his mythical 'ownership' in the company. Imagine you had a $100,000 term life insurance policy from a mutual company. Do you think you could sell your ownership in that company? The answer, Mrs. Easymark, is no, and if you tried, they'd put you in a rubber room!"

Now Connie was giving Don her full attention. "There must be something policyholders can do about that financial fast shuffle!"

"There is. According to the ideas advanced in *The Billion Dollar Bookies*, mutual policyholders stand to gain $20,000 or more for their share of the company. It's a true education."

"Which book blows the whistle on the stock companies?"

Don took another book from the shelf. "This is it." He handed her *Life Insurance and the Public Interest* by the late Halsey Josephson, C.L.U., a Chartered Life Underwriter, author of four insurance books and former regular columnist for three major life insurance publications. "This book is a challenge to read because Halsey Josephson spoke flawless insurancese. He probably even knew what 'Flitcraft' means.

"Josephson says he wrote this book 'to convince the life insurance buying public and our legislators that stock life insurance is undesirable socially and economically, is inimical to the best interests of the community and is a bootless waste of policyholders' money.' 'Bootless' is defined in the *American Heritage Dictionary* as: 'Useless; Fruitless; Unavailing and having no advantage or benefit.'"

Connie thought before commenting. "Both authors are experts on the subject. It seems both types of companies are working some kind of scam mainly to grab control and use of other people's money. And all on a pretext of performing an important service."

"It certainly looks that way, Connie. Anyone who bothers

25

to read these books will learn of the devious schemes to siphon off company assets through mergers and financial trickery without going to jail. Josephson says executives of both stock and mutual companies cooperate to resist regulations and legislation created to control what he calls 'the prerogatives of management.'"

"The prerogatives of insurance management," Connie concluded, "are liable to create serious problems for small investors and that coveted policyholder, John Q. Sucker."

"Spoken like a true Easymark," said Don.

LIFE INSURANCE IS LIGHT

Donald T. sat back to read *Life Insurance Is Light*, a thick, red leather-bound book with the title printed in gold leaf on the spine. The author, Darwin P. Kingsley, was president of New York Life Insurance Company back in the early 1900s.

"Connie," said Don, "I'll bet you didn't know that life insurance is light."

"No, I wasn't aware of that."

He handed her the book. She thumbed through the pages. "Jeepers! This is in stilted, celluloid-collar language."

"That's because it was written in the 1920s and Mr. Kingsley tends to mix insurancese with English."

"Just listen to what it says on page 36." She read the following passage:

> A mutual life insurance company is the only perfect democracy in the world, if perfection can be claimed for anything human.

"Everything looks like a perfect democracy when you're sitting on top of a skyscraper full of other people's money," Connie reasoned.

"Now, Connie," Don joked, "you're being critical of a big business executive with broad vision who knows something he doesn't want us peasants to know."

"You'd be critical too if you read what else it says on this same page." Connie read on:

The whole fabric of a mutual company almost shouts the self-evident truth that men are created unequal.

"I've always wondered about that," Don said.

"Well, wonder no longer. He explains it right here in his own language." She continued reading:

...and yet, paradoxical as it may seem to those who believe in the Jeffersonian dogma, mutual life insurance, denying the natural equality of men, denying the truth of Jefferson's declaration, has created a true democracy, a democracy of which our fathers dreamed, for which they fought, within which the right to life, liberty and the pursuit of happiness cannot be invaded.

"That's just another spooky statement!" Don exclaimed. "I don't see how it explains why men are created unequal."

Connie continued turning the pages. "This is heavy, heavy, heavy! It says this book was put out for the 'delectation and perhaps inspiration' of New York Life Insurance Company men and women."

"We're lucky that guy isn't alive today, he'd upchuck that stuff all over the viewers on national television. Let me show you what arrived in the mail this morning — it makes Darwin P. Kingsley look like an amateur. It's the best bullshit of the month!"

BEST BULLSHIT OF THE MONTH

Don opened his mail box and was taken aback by a blast of thunderous flatulence. The following form letter on the letterhead of Pioneer Life Insurance Company of Illinois was sent to G.R.I.M. by an outraged victim:

```
Cert. No. _____

Dear Mr. _____:


    In spite of continuing dramatic
increases in the cost of health care, I
am pleased to tell you that there will
not be a general rate increase in your
Keystone Group coverage during the
remainder of 1982. I am certain you
have heard from friends and relatives
that most companies have found it neces-
sary to increase premiums substantially
— sometimes double what they recently
were.
    Rather than increase premium rates,
we will institute a $7.50 monthly
administrative fee. The fee will be
included with all premium billings and
```

pre-authorized checks due on and after October 1, 1982.

This modest fee — less than 25¢ per day — will help offset the cost of policy administration and allow a continuation of your valuable protection at present premium rates. We know your Keystone Group health plan ranks on a par with your life insurance program in your overall financial security planning. We are happy to make it available to you. Please be assured that we are always ready to serve all your life, health and accident needs.

Sincerely,

Vice President
Administrative Group Services

P.S. We have enclosed your new personalized Policyholder Identification Card. Please read the instructions for its use on the reverse side and sign your name in the space provided.

"Well," Connie commented, "that should keep your garden fertilized until the next rate increase!"

"Well, Emma, your idea to mix all them insurance ads into the
fertilizer sure has perked up these posies!"

TOP PRIORITY
(Time Sensitive Material)

Don's mailbox was flooded with offers of pie-in-the-sky financial protection. He had responded in Connie's name to a T.V. pitch offering life insurance for people over forty-five for "as little as $5 a month." His rash response produced an oversized envelope addressed to Connie Easymark. For several reasons, this gigantic mailer stood out from the other junk mail:

1. "TOP PRIORITY" was printed on a wide red stripe at both ends of the enormous envelope.
2. "IMPORTANT MESSAGE ENCLOSED FOR MS. CONNIE EASYMARK FROM T.V.'s MICHAEL LANDON" was below the address in red computer type.
3. "URGENT NOTIFICATION FOR CONNIE EASY-MARK" was printed where the return address is usually imprinted.
4. Like a hastily applied hand stamp with a red border, a message at the lower left corner of the envelope read, "TIME SENSITIVE MATERIAL, PLEASE OPEN AT ONCE."
5. Also on the front was the notation, "Ms. Connie Easymark, the enclosed benefit tags are made out in your name only. Select one and return for two months coverage at no cost to you."

6. On the back of the envelope was, "4 BONUS BENE-
   FIT TAGS MADE OUT EXCLUSIVELY FOR CONNIE
   EASYMARK ENCLOSED. CHOOSE ONLY ONE."

"Connie, you really have a frantic message here. It's
urgent, top priority, time sensitive, with bonus benefit tags in
your name only...and enclosed is an important message for
you from T.V.'s Michael Landon."
"Read it for me, please."

"Get the ball bat, Lois! It's another one of those You Can't Be
Turned Down, Guaranteed Acceptance *pitches."*

He opened the envelope and read for a few minutes. "They want you to buy life insurance with a 'Triple Guarantee' promising that your premium rate will not increase as you grow older."

"I'm glad to hear that. I can breathe easier now."

"The premium doesn't increase but the benefits get smaller as you get older. Benefits decrease to as little as $700 if death occurs after age seventy. Subtract from that premiums already paid in and you might wish you'd put your money in a savings account — or maybe even a cigar box!"

"They feed us a lot of Madison Avenue stuff, Don, when they promise premiums won't increase as you grow older! Any idiot can figure out that less benefits for the premium dollar means premiums have gone up!"

Don continued, "During the first two years of coverage there are no benefits, only return of paid premiums if death results from anything other than accidental bodily injury. The policy is underwritten by Academy Life Insurance Company, operating out of their towering headquarters in Valley Forge, Pennsylvania."

Connie's only comment was, "Shades of Honest-George-Washington-who-couldn't-tell-a-lie! I wonder where they ever found enough money to build towering headquarters in Valley Forge."

Don said, "I think T.V. commercials that recommend that stuff to gullible viewers are partially responsible. Remember the old saying, 'He who holds the ladder is as guilty as the thief.'"

LEGISLATIVE HULAS
(Hawaiian Auto Insurance)

Don Easymark turned on the television, then sat back in his favorite chair to watch the evening news. The grim-visaged newscaster announced, "Organized crime is causing insurance rates to rise in the city."

"Damnit! What'll they think of next." Don shut off the T.V. "There is a limit to how much of that bilge the human mind will accept!"

"Actually, that's not bilge, it's fact," exclaimed Connie. "Some companies charge up to $8,129 for $162 worth of auto insurance and that's definitely organized crime!"

She was talking about a full-page ad placed in the January 28, 1981, *Honolulu Advertiser* by the State Insurance Regulatory Office. Annual rates ranged from $162 to $8,129 for the compulsory coverage depending, of course, on the buyers' success in finding out who's selling what, for how much, to whom! In Hawaii, liability insurance is required by law for over half-a-million motor vehicles and that's captive business for the insurance industry.

Connie theorized, "The six- and eight-thousand-dollar auto insurance rates are probably a devious way of saying they refuse to insure anyone with two speeding convictions — deception is the backbone of the business. On the other hand, one or all of the actuaries, typesetters or proofreaders may

Portion of a full-page ad in the *Honolulu Advertiser* (checks added to emphasize actuarial hallucinations)

Company (Alphabetical order)	Terr. Use	OAHU To/From Pleasure	Work	MAUI To/From Pleasure	Work	KAUAI To/From Pleasure	Work	HAWAII To/From Pleasure	Work
2 SPEEDING & 1 MOVING CONVICTIONS									
Aetna Casualty & Surety Co.		1,047	1,114	987	1,044	904	957	939	995
Aetna Fire Underwriters Ins. Co.		393	452	343	394	301	346	346	398
Aetna Insurance Co.		393	452	343	394	301	346	346	398
Allstate Indemnity Co.		1,272	1,398	1,058	1,176	920	1,020	1,078	1,194
Allstate Insurance Co.		796	876	664	736	578	640	672	744
American Alliance Insurance Co.		318	354	210	235	209	234	243	273
American Automobile Insurance Co.		992	1,090	672	738	758	830	764	838
American Casualty Co. of Reading, PA		247	284	188	216	187	200	224	257
American Employers' Insurance Co.		709	775	528	579	516	565	609	700
American & Foreign Insurance Co.		451	518	410	472	354	407	409	470
American Home Assurance Co.		596	684	436	501	438	502	500	575
American Insurance Co.		992	1,090	672	738	758	830	764	838
American Manufacturers Mutual Ins. Co.		400	459	328	377	289	333	330	379
American Motorists Ins. Co.		400	459	328	377	289	333	330	379
American Mutual Liability Ins. Co.		370	425	236	271	236	271	261	300
American National Fire Ins. Co.		318	354	210	235	209	234	243	273
American Star Insurance Co.		252	290	178	204	178	204	207	237
Amica Mutual Insurance Co.		249	286	177	203	176	201	207	237
Argonaut Insurance Co.		548	608	468	520	410	458	470	532
Argonaut-Midwest Insurance Co.		548	608	468	520	410	458	470	532
Associated Indemnity Corp.		992	1,090	672	738	758	830	764	838
Assurance Company of America		422	484	300	346	298	344	360	416
Bishop Insurance of Hawaii, Inc.		709	775	528	579	516	565	609	700
Carriers Insurance Co.		315	362	224	257	222	255	274	314
Centennial Insurance Co.		247	284	176	202	175	200	206	236
Charter Oak Fire Insurance Co.		1,397	1,505	1,043	1,130	1,023	1,109	1,238	1,343
City Insurance Co.		378	434	329	377	291	334	333	382
Colonial Penn Insurance Co.		697	893	491	630	472	605	591	757
Commercial Ins. Co. of Newark, N.J.		1,164	1,267	979	1,065	946	1,029	1,012	1,102
Commercial Union Ins. Co.		709	775	528	579	516	565	609	700
Continental Casualty Co.		247	284	188	216	187	200	224	257
Continental Insurance Co.		1,164	1,267	979	1,065	946	1,029	1,012	1,102
Continental Reinsurance Corp.		1,164	1,267	979	1,065	946	1,029	1,012	1,102
Criterion Insurance Co.		2,822	2,918	1,982	2,030	1,982	2,030	2,058	2,114
Cumis Insurance Society, Inc.		997	1,057	917	972	828	877	870	921
Employers' Fire Insurance Co.		709	775	528	579	516	565	609	700
Employers' Insurance of Wausau		679	793	637	743	569	664	601	700
Federal Insurance Co.		482	554	434	499	352	404	434	498
Fidelity & Casualty Co. of New York		1,164	1,267	979	1,065	946	1,029	1,012	1,102
Financial Security Insurance Co.		1,518	1,586	1,388	1,494	1,246	1,382	1,318	1,406
Fireman's Fund Ins. Co.		992	1,090	672	738	758	830	764	838
Fireman's Ins. Co. of Newark, N.J.		1,164	1,267	979	1,065	946	1,029	1,012	1,102
First Insurance Co. of Hawaii, Ltd.		1,164	1,267	979	1,065	946	1,029	1,012	1,102
General Accident Fire & Life Assurance		290	334	211	243	209	240	249	286
Glens Falls Insurance Co.		1,164	1,267	979	1,065	946	1,029	1,012	1,102
Globe Indemnity Co.		451	518	410	472	354	407	409	470
Government Employees Insurance Co.		1,314	1,364	917	1,016	973	1,011	1,166	1,200
Grain Dealers Mutual Insurance Co.		2,680	2,781	1,808	1,876	1,784	1,852	2,365	2,457
Great American Ins. Co.		318	354	210	235	209	234	243	273
Gulf Insurance Co.		523	581	486	539	438	486	457	508
Hartford Accident & Indemnity Co.		980	1,042	706	750	700	742	858	910
Hawaiian Insurance & Guaranty Co., Ltd.		976	1,050	634	684	630	680	740	798
Highlands Insurance Co.		466	504	332	397	329	393	389	458
Home Indemnity Co.		378	434	329	377	291	334	333	382
Home Insurance Co.		378	434	329	377	291	334	333	382
Ideal Mutual Ins. Co.		220	253	160	184	158	182	188	216
Industrial Indemnity Co.		898	981	835	914	752	823	787	861
Industrial Indemnity Co. of the Northwest		898	981	835	914	752	823	787	861
Industrial Insurance Co.		898	981	835	914	752	823	787	861
Industrial Insurance Co. of Hawaii		898	981	835	914	752	823	787	861
Industrial Underwriters Insurance Co.		898	981	835	914	752	823	787	861
Inland National Insurance Co.		341	391	295	339	260	299	299	344
Insurance Co. of North America		427	491	401	461	361	415	377	433
Insurance Company of the State of PA.		341	391	295	339	260	299	299	344

36

Honolulu Advertiser   Wednesday, January 21, 1981

Company (Alphabetical order)	Terr. Use	OAHU		MAUI		KAUAI		HAWAII	
		Pleasure	Work To/From	Pleasure	Work To/From	Pleasure	Work To/From	Pleasure	Work To/From
2 SPEEDING & 1 MOVING CONVICTIONS									
International Service Insurance Co.		529	588	387	431	382	426	432	480
Island Insurance Co.		1,285	1,360	1,202	1,274	1,071	1,133	1,128	1,195
Liberty Mutual Fire Insurance Co.		1,063	1,115	771	816	762	804	806	851
Liberty Mutual Insurance Co.		372	426	312	356	278	323	321	370
Lumbermens Mutual Casualty Co.		400	459	328	377	289	333	330	379
Maryland Casualty Co.		422	484	300	346	298	344	360	416
Michigan Mutual Insurance Co.		242	279	174	200	172	197	203	233
Midland Insurance Co.		249	285	159	182	158	181	186	213
National Fire Ins. Co. of Hartford		247	284	188	216	187	200	224	257
National Surety Corp.		992	1,090	672	738	758	830	764	838
National Union Fire Ins. Co. of Pittsburgh, PA.		782	898	548	630	550	632	630	723
Nationwide Mutual Insurance Co.		224	247	172	190	172	190	177	196
New Hampsire Insurance Co.		341	391	295	339	260	299	299	344
New York Underwriters Ins. Co.		980	1,042	706	750	700	742	858	910
Newark Insurance Co.		451	518	410	472	354	407	409	470
North River Insurance Co.		898	981	835	914	752	823	787	861
Northbrook Property & Casualty Ins. Co.		796	876	664	736	578	640	672	744
Northern Assurance Co.		709	775	528	579	516	565	609	700
Northern Ins. Co. of New York		422	484	300	346	298	344	360	416
Northwestern National Ins. Co.		469	539	434	500	392	451	411	473
Pacific Employers Ins. Co.		427	491	401	461	361	415	377	433
Pacific Indemnity Co.		482	554	434	499	352	404	434	498
Pacific Insurance Co., Ltd.		980	1,042	706	750	700	742	858	910
Phoenix Insurance Co.		931	1,003	695	753	682	739	825	895
Premier Insurance Co.		740	818	588	651	523	578	599	663
Ranger Insurance Co.		243	279	174	199	171	195	203	233
Reliance Insurance Co.		249	286	177	203	176	201	207	237
Royal Indemnity Co.		451	518	410	472	354	407	409	470
Royal Insurance Co. of America		451	518	410	472	354	407	409	470
Safeguard Insurance Co.		451	518	410	472	354	407	409	470
St. Paul Fire & Marine Ins. Co.		524	602	487	559	438	504	464	533
Sentinel Insurance Co.		980	1,042	706	750	700	742	858	910
Sentry Insurance A Mutual Co.		584	672	373	428	371	424	438	502
Standard Fire Insurance Co.		1,047	1,114	987	1,044	904	957	939	995
State Farm Fire & Casualty Co.		1,282	1,512	1,297	1,530	1,008	1,189	1,080	1,274
State Farm General Insurance Co.		7,883	8,033	7,978	8,129	6,187	6,304	6,638	6,764
State Farm Mutual Auto Insurance Co.		3,189	3,765	3,179	3,753	2,471	2,916	2,699	3,185
Tokio Marine & Fire Insurance Co.		948	1,023	704	759	700	755	850	916
Tradewind Insurance Co.		1,285	1,360	1,202	1,274	1,071	1,133	1,128	1,195
Transamerica Insurance Co.		777	859	617	684	549	607	629	696
Transit Casualty Co.		420	482	299	344	294	338	358	411
Transport Indemnity Co.		243	279	173	198	171	195	202	231
Transport Insurance Co.		376	432	267	307	264	303	327	376
Transportation Insurance Co.		247	284	188	216	187	200	224	257
Travelers Indemnity Co.		931	1,003	695	753	682	739	825	895
Travelers Indemnity Co. of America		931	1,003	695	753	682	739	825	895
Travelers Indemnity Co. of Illinois		931	1,003	695	753	682	739	825	895
Travelers Indemnity Co. of Rhode Island		931	1,003	695	753	682	739	825	895
Travelers Insurance Co.		931	1,003	695	753	682	739	825	895
Truck Insurance Exchange		220	253	141	162	139	160	164	188
United National Ins. Co., Ltd.		976	1,050	634	684	630	680	740	798
United Pacific Insurance Co.		249	286	177	203	176	201	207	237
United Services Automobile Association		885	982	673	745	631	694	697	770
USAA Casualty Insurance Co.		790	874	600	665	563	624	625	691
United States Fidelity & Guaranty Co.		238	275	168	193	167	191	196	225
United States Fire Insurance Co.		898	981	835	914	752	823	787	861
Universal Reinsurance Corporation		469	539	434	500	392	451	411	473
Universal Underwriters Insurance Co.		241	277	173	198	170	194	201	231
Utica Mutual Insurance Co.		931	986	799	845	707	747	810	856
Westchester Fire Insurance Co.		898	981	835	914	752	823	787	861
Western Employers Insurance Company		228	262	167	192	165	189	197	226
Zurich Insurance Co.		495	569	449	516	391	449	448	515

have been smoking some of that exotic Hawaiian tobacco that grows between the rows of sugarcane."

"The insurance moguls have it pretty good slopping it up at the Hawaiian motor vehicle trough," Don snorted. "I'll bet they paid the lawmakers a commission for that 'buy-insurance-or-else' legislative hula."

"Paying a commission would be illegal, Don, but I'll bet they slipped the senators a few coconuts under the table — or maybe a few free insurance policies and maybe even some low interest mortgages or business loans."

"Amen to that, Connie! Lawmakers incur obligations through acceptance of services as surely as through cash pay-offs."

Connie grumbled, "I've had insurance for breakfast, lunch and dinner. I'm not sure I want to talk about it anymore."

"I don't blame you," Don grinned, "but I'll bet you'd like to hear something about a really big can of insurance worms, like the assigned risk racket."

"OK, you may proceed, but keep it brief."

ASSIGNED RISK
(A License To Steal?)

Why do you call the assigned risk system a can of worms?" Connie asked. "I always thought it was a wonderful plan to help people obtain auto insurance when they'd been refused coverage by some desk-bound underwriter in compliance with his company's instructions."

"I really shouldn't have called it a can of worms. That was inaccurate. I should have called it a legalized racket of *alarming* magnitude."

"Interesting, if true. So alarm me a little."

"OK, read this news release that came in the mail from the New Jersey Insurance Department. In addition to the usual rate increases blessed by the commissioner, it says New Jersey has about 1.4-million cars in the assigned risk category."

Connie read the release twice and said, "My goodness, 1.4 million is an unbelievably large number of dangerous drivers for such a small state."

"According to the almanac, Connie, there are at least 4,284,000 automobiles in New Jersey. About a third of those cars are being stuck with huge assigned risk premiums, many well over $1,000 annually."

"Is the industry trying to say that almost one out of every three New Jersey drivers is some kind of drunken, wild-eyed

STATE OF NEW JERSEY OFFICIAL NEWS RELEASE

DEPARTMENT OF INSURANCE

Joseph F. Murphy, Commissioner For information contact:

Phone: Trenton (609) 292-6499

Thomas J. Hooper

FOR RELEASE January 31, 1983

TRENTON - The seven per cent increase in auto insurance rates for the 200 companies of the Insurance Services Office, which took effect January 11, will be adopted by the New Jersey Automobile Insurance Plan (Assigned Risk), effective January 31 for new business and March 2 for renewals, State Insurance Commissioner Joseph F. Murphy said today.

It has long been the policy in New Jersey, Murphy noted, that the NJAIP use the rates approved for the ISO and that increases granted to ISO are historically used by the NJAIP. There are about 1.4 million cars in the assigned risk category.

menace on the highway?" Connie asked. "I find that hard to believe. Could it be that the companies are using the assigned risk system as a license to steal and bilk motorists state-wide?"

"Bilk is a good word," Don replied. "People can defend themselves against traffic citations in court, but there's absolutely no way they can defend themselves against the assigned risk shell game."

Don had been fleeced by the assigned risk system in the past. "Hell, Connie," he said, "you don't have to be a wobbly-legged drunk driver with your eyes crossed and your tongue hanging out the side of your mouth to be shafted by the assigned risk system! You can be classified as an assigned risk at the slightest provocation. They seize on anything as an excuse to uprate you. In California, you can be charged extra for failing to buy auto insurance for the past sixty days! Cold-sober, law-abiding people everywhere have been labeled 'assigned risks.' Typical assigned risk victims have been Hispanics, blacks, actors, students, bartenders, divorced people, agricultural workers, professional athletes, people living in the 'wrong' neighborhood and anyone else they can accuse of not being up to insurance 'standards.'"

"I don't think the assigned risk system is up to the 'standards' of the motoring public," Connie commented. "It sounds more like a gigantic white collar crime than a true service to the nation's motorists."

"It's a crime by any standard. The color of their collars has nothing to do with it. Extorting sky-high 'assigned risk' premiums from motorists based on where they work or where they sleep at night is just another way to profit unfairly.

NEW JERSEY BUS STOP IN JANUARY

"My agent says I owe more than a month's pay for my assigned risk auto insurance.... I wonder when the bus will get here."

People with safe driving records should not be penalized for where they work or live.

"California Assembly Bill #731 would have stamped out assigned risk swindles. It was one of the most carefully researched auto insurance bills ever written, so true to form, insurance lobbyists squelched it out of existence. AB-731 provided for liability insurance to be automatically included with gas at the pump. People with two or more cars would pay for insurance only on cars being driven at the time, not on cars sitting in the garage.

"All drivers would be covered with liability insurance through a special state treasury fund created by a 6 percent fuel tax along with specified registration and license fees. Traffic violators would be penalized by the courts and not by four-digit assigned risk overcharges. The more people drove the more they would pay and, quite properly, the less they drove the less they would pay. The bill was not an industry windfall, so with total disregard for the public interest, it was blocked by the robber barons.

"Similar legislation is being studied in California. Hopefully, someday such legislation will be enacted nationally."

Cheer up, Mr. Assigned Risk. Doctors all agree,
walking is good for you!

$125,000 HOME FOR ONLY $457,485
(Easy Money For Insurers)

"**R**eal estate mortgages are sometimes called financial 'instruments,'" said Don. "I think they should be called financial 'shafts'! If John Q. Sucker put a $25,000 down payment on a $125,000 home to shelter his wife and kids, and paid his mortgage faithfully according to its terms and conditions, how much money would be screwed out of him by the private insurance industry?"

"Gee, I don't know," Connie said, "let's figure it out."

"OK, here's the handy-dandy solar-powered pocket calculator. I'll give you the numbers and you total them."

Don reached for a book of mortgage amortization tables. "Regardless of where mortgage loans are transacted," he said, "at a bank, mortgage company, credit union or wherever, they usually end up being 'packaged' with other mortgages and sold wholesale to the *investment department of some insurance company or an insurance company masquerading as a gung ho 'financial corporation.'* Insurance companies refuse to buy mortgages unless they are self-serving, highly profitable to the lender and brutal to the borrower; I guess you know that."

"Of course I know it. I worked for a mortgage company once, remember?"

"Let's assume that to buy a $125,000 home Mr. Sucker had to borrow $100,000 at 13.5 percent for thirty years." Don looked at the amortization book. "Egad! The payments would be $1,145 per month! Multiply that by 360 months; deduct the borrowed $100,000 and log the rest in the total payola column."

Connie poked the calculator keys. "That would be $412,200 minus $100,000 — a total of $312,200 extra for loaning $100,000 worth of policyholders' money to J.Q. Sucker."

"Let's list the rest of the money weaseled out of this deal. Add another $3,000 because they could refuse to make poor old J.Q.'s loan unless the seller pays a 3-point discount. Three 'points' means 3 percent in insurancese. How does that grab you?"

"That's rotten. It brings the total to $315,000 extra."

"Well, they don't stop there. They'll refuse to make the loan unless John Q. agrees, under penalty of foreclosure, to keep the home covered with fire insurance and extended coverage for the term of the loan. That would be $6,750 at today's rates and proportionally more with the inevitable rate increases. Most policies also charge to cover the non-inflammable ground beneath the home!"

"Protective, but high on the irritation scale. That totals $321,750 extra. Wow — that should keep them in paperclips for a while!"

"Here's another entry for your irritation scale: They'll refuse to make Mr. Sucker's loan unless someone pays $585 for a $125,000 title insurance policy to guarantee against undetected liens or other encumbrances against the property."

"This is uncivilized! It brings the payola total to $322,385 extra!"

Don said, "They check the title by computer in a matter of seconds, then demand $585! According to *The Screwing Of The Average Man* by David Hapgood, title companies pay out only 2.5 percent of their income in benefits. This means the $585 represents an average benefit of $14.63! In order to rationalize such a windfall, the companies argue that title research is expensive. They warn that old Spanish land grants might

STATE-OF-THE-ART TITLE INSURANCE MACHINE
(Feed it $585 and it excretes $14.63 in benefits!)

cloud real estate titles."

"Horrors, I wouldn't want some old Spaniard trying to take my house away — and you can quote me on that!"

Don continued, "If Mr. Sucker bought his house through one of those national real estate corporations like Century 21 that has been bought out by some insurance company seeking to control the mortgage financing, there would be a 7 percent commission. Add another $8,750."

"Now the total is a whopping $331,085! We wouldn't want them to be caught short, would we?"

"Don't worry about that," Don replied. "The seller has to give clear title, so he will have to pay off the existing mortgage. A balance of $70,000 could call for a 2 percent prepayment penalty. Add another $1,400."

"That totals $332,485 over and above what the house cost to begin with! This is clearly a case where private enterprise does it worse!"

"It's simple," said Don. "Any American can buy a $125,000 home on terms if he doesn't mind giving back over three times the total amount he borrowed. The nightmare begins when the fine-print jockeys launch into a pompous, holier-than-thou financial ritual to milk an additional $332,485 out of the poor guy's transaction. This huge additional charge pays for only three relatively simple services: 1) Helping to arrange an agreement between buyer and seller; 2) Loaning out $100,000 of someone else's money; 3) Handing out pieces of paper called 'policies' containing promises that can be rendered meaningless by well-researched escape clauses and exclusions."

"Squeezing a total of $432,485 back out of a piddling $100,000 loan," said Connie, "is clear proof of either outrageous thievery or inexcusable inefficiency."

"Mr. Sucker would have been in worse trouble if he had signed one of those tricky 'Adjustable Rate' mortgages (A.R.M.s)," Don went on. "A.R.M. interest rates fluctuate, causing burdensome and often unaffordable increases in monthly payments. In the early 1980s there were an estimated 150 different A.R.M.s available with virtually no standardization of terms. In some cases payments went up even when the prime rate went down!"

He picked up a copy of the *Los Angeles Times* and read, "In Los Angeles County alone, foreclosures increased from 1,280 in 1980 to 11,810 in 1983."

"Can you imagine," he said, "the modern-day Simon Legrees twirled their mustaches and foreclosed on 11,810 Los Angeles victims! Mr. Sucker is better off with his existing fixed rate mortgage because he doesn't have to be some kind of fortuneteller to predict what it's going to cost him."

"He's better off in the same way that it's better to be raped than murdered," was Connie's conclusion.

"Almost every home and commercial building in the nation has a mortgage on it," said Don. "Small wonder the economy is always out of balance and we have perpetual inflation. After World War II nice homes sold for $12,000 and mortgage lenders became wealthy charging 4 percent and 5 percent interest, while little men in green eyeshades were paid a living wage to do the accounting. In the early 1980s, with homes selling for more than $100,000, they gouged and extorted 13 percent interest and often more, while unsalaried computers did the basic accounting. In late 1986 headlines *bragged* that thirty-year conventional loan rates had dropped to 9.98 percent. That rate on a mortgage would have gotten them laughed out of town in saner times!"

Don tossed the amortization book into the desk drawer. "Those financial geniuses in the insurance boardrooms should give serious thought to the old saying, 'Little piggies come home to feed again, but big hogs get slaughtered.'"

"Except when they own the slaughterhouse," Connie added.

"Owning the slaughterhouse may not save them this time. Their greed is coming home to roost. There is a rash of foreclosures nationwide. Houston, Texas, is called 'Foreclosure City, U.S.A.' The paper says For Sale signs are as common as Stetson hats. The Houston Foreclosure Listing Service reported 2,486 foreclosures in the month of September 1985!

That's a 2,052 increase over the 434 foreclosures in Houston in September 1980. Some victims were lured, with artificially low interest rates, into signing adjustable rate mortgages where interest rates skyrocketed to unaffordable levels. Meanwhile, not only in Houston but nationwide, people by the thousands are losing their homes while the insurance industry, responsible for the tragedy to begin with, lurks piously and anonymously in the background."

FINANCIAL SUPERMARKETS
(Step Right Up, Folks, And Bring Money)

"**W**hat are these 'financial supermarkets' the big insurance companies are touting?" Connie asked.

"I only know what I read in the papers," said Don. "It seems people no longer accept the old wheeze about cash value life insurance being a good value for the money.

"Major insurance companies purchase control of banks, large national stock brokerages, savings & loans and real estate corporations. Most of these businesses create a need to borrow money and all attract borrowers. They can be used to sell financial schemes that are difficult to understand but suggest profits for the public. Enticed by profit, victims ask few questions. Legitimate and ethical financial planners suffer when white collar thieves masquerade as 'financial advisers.' Insurers use their powerful political influence for self-serving activities, like lobbying through an amendment to the Federal Trade Commission Act prohibiting the FTC from ever studying insurance. This leaves people without effective protection. It leaves nearly 2,000 smaller insurance companies in a noncompetitive and weak position — an easy takeover for the big companies. Actually, this is free enterprise dangerously out of control."

"Out of control is an understatement," said Connie. "The

"There you have it, gentlemen, our cradle-to-grave financial supermarkets will be firmly entrenched by the time big government figures this out!"

morning paper says Prudential's assets dwarf the total wealth of many Third World countries."

"We peasants aren't supposed to think about things like that," said Don. "The magnitude of it boggles the mind. I don't know what the greedy bastards think they're going to do with all that money other than control free enterprise and buy political power they shouldn't have in the first place. They're even into the 'Let's Play Banker' game and are trying to muscle into the banking business because banking simplifies controlling other people's money."

"If banking in the future is as unprincipled as the

insurance industry of the past," Connie added, "we're in deep, deep trouble."

"We're already in deep kim-chee," said Don. "Nothing says it better than this letter to the paper from a resident of Redondo Beach, California." He handed her the letter:

GREED IS RUINING INDUSTRIAL BASE

Lester Thurow's Viewpoint, "U.S. Can't Compete If Finance Continues as the Master of Industry," shows how our current business leaders have discovered the convenience of manipulating for profit rather than the out-dated method of producing for profit.

The greed now rampant in our business community is destroying the solid industrial base that required generations to build and the work ethic is rapidly becoming a meaningless concept.

We need legislation to stop future leveraged buy-outs and to prevent America from becoming a debtor's paradise and an industrial wasteland.

Sir John Glubb in his *The Fate of Empires* concluded that great civilizations have a life cycle of about 250 years and that great nations usually fall due to internal reasons alone. As the United States approaches year 250, let us hope that the maneuvering of industrial financiers is not allowed to continue.

Roger A. Evans
Redondo Beach

"Greed for money obliterates the industrial financiers' sense of values. They ought to read 'The Strangest Planet Of All,' written by Art Hoppe back in the sixties," said Connie. She rummaged through her keepsakes and handed Don a copy.

THE STRANGEST PLANET OF ALL
by Art Hoppe

The starship NX8307, Captain Xenon commanding, returned safely to her home base on Arcturus IV and the captain, looking somewhat nervous, strode to the Council of Wise Elders to make his report.

"Well, Captain," said the Eldest Elder, "did you find a planet we might colonize and exploit?"

"I think so, sir," said Captain Xenon uneasily. "Terra, the third planet out from Sol. A lovely green world. True, the atmosphere is thick with carbon monoxide, but breathable. The waters are turgid with pollutants, but purifiable, and the inhabitants are bellicose and a little mad, but basically lovable."

"It sounds colonizable, Captain. But is it exploitable? What do these natives make?"

"Money, sir. From the cradle to the grave, the primary drive of each native is to make as much money as possible."

"Ah," said the Eldest Elder, "they have discovered a precious asset worth striving for. Tell us, Captain, what is money?"

Here the Captain frowned. "It's a little difficult to explain, sir."

"Come, come, Captain. Is it edible, drinkable, wearable, lethal or purely aesthetic?"

"No, sir. It's... Well, it's pieces of paper."

"Paper, Captain?"

"Yes, sir. They toil, lie, cheat, steal, kill and war for it. But that's because it represents gold."

"Oh yes, that soft, yellow metal. They've found some use for gold, other than filling teeth?"

"No, sir. It's intrinsically worthless, too, but they dig it up out of the ground and then bury it under the ground. They believe this makes the pieces of paper valuable."

"Just a minute, Captain..."

"At the moment, sir, the whole planet is in crisis because the leading nation state has less worthless gold buried underground than it used to have, and they fear this might make the worthless paper money worthless, in which case millions will starve because..."

"Control yourself, please, Captain."

"...because each native values the paper only because all other natives value it. And should their faith in this worthless paper be destroyed, they would stop producing food, clothing and shelter because they'd have nothing worthless to strive for and..."

At this point, Captain Xenon had to be forcibly restrained. And he was led off babbling something about 35 pieces of paper per ounce, Arab sheiks, General de Gaulle, seven bankers, dual pricing, gold pools and other hallucinatory nonsense.

The Council of Wise Elders then voted unanimously to bypass Terra and instead colonize Betalgeuse XIV, where the mauve-colored three-headed inhabitants devoted their lives to making pistachio ice cream.

"When it comes to money," said the Eldest Elder wisely, "let's take pistachio."

Don said, "No doubt the insurance establishment on Betalgeuse XIV found a way to snatch a controlling interest in most of the pistachio ice cream up there!"

Herbert A. McArbitrage III
(Of the Prudential Bache McArbitrages)

ARBITRAGE: [L. arbitrari] simultaneous purchase and sale of the same or equivalent security in order to profit from price discrepancies (one way to make millions with policy-holders' cash).

Donald T. Easymark answered one of Prudential Bache's more intriguing advertisements...with the following result:.

Phone	Burp... Burp...
Don	Hello, Don Easymark speaking.
Caller	This is Herb McArbitrage at Bache, Mr. Easymark.
Don	Oh yes...
Herb	(garbled) some information you saw on T.V. in July.
Don	Yes...
Herb	OK, I just wanted to check with you and see...talk about capitalizing on taxes. Do you buy investments now with tax-free advantages on?
Don	No, we don't.
Herb	OK, do you buy utilities?
Don	No. We responded to that T.V. pitch just because we were curious as to what the situation was.
Herb	Ah-huh... (pause.) Well, it goes without saying that... uh...right now there are utilities that collect high yields and you re-invest those dividend checks back into the

	company and you get tax-free status. Ah...uh...$1,500 per couple or $750 per individual — tax-free each year. That's what one part of the law is all about.
Don	I see...
Herb	And uh... of course as far as I'm concerned, where interest rates are right now, we've got people coming out of the money markets left and right... People going long term would like another yield before interest rates start coming down, which they already have to some extent. But...ah...the question is, have you invested in securities at all before?
Don	Not to any extent, no.
Herb	Ah-hah... Well, really, that's what that was all about. I just thought I'd check back with you and see if... do you know the San Diego Gas & Electric preferred that came out a few days ago?
Don	Yes.
Herb	It was yield at 16 7/8 percent... Well, that thing's already going at a premium now — meaning people that bought at $27.50 would now have to pay $28.25! The reason for that is the yield is so high and when it starts coming down...somebody latches on to those high yields now...they've got everything going for 'em!
Don	Don't you think the bubble will burst someday?
Herb	On those yields?
Don	Yes.
Herb	Well, yes... Interest rates have to come down. But that doesn't...that won't have any effect on...any effect the things out that's (unintelligible).
Don	We are particularly interested in the big insurance companies that are buying up the largest national stock brokerage houses —
Herb	Ah-hah...
Don	We would like to know what is going to happen when the big boys like Allstate, Metropolitan, Prudential and Equitable have bought all the stock brokerage houses, leaving 2,000 small insurers without a brokerage house to launder their money in? They won't even

	be able to manipulate the market. What's going to happen then?
Herb	Well, that's a fair question... It's the same old story, the big fish crowding out the little ones. I'd...er...imagine the little insurance companies would be able to start merging into the bigger ones —
Don	(snicker)
Herb	— all it says is that there are going to be fewer companies doing that kind of thing, but it will still be very competitive...but...but
Don	Fewer companies servicing us bigger and better?
Herb	Right. That's all.
Don	Yeah... Well, OK, Mr. McArbitrage, thank you very much for calling.
Herb	You are most welcome.
Don	Goodbye.

Donald hung up the phone and said to Connie, "It's a free society, so I guess it's OK for the big fish to crowd out the little fish when they're not relieving people of their money. Hell, Sears Roebuck even used to sell opium to the peasants back in the 1800s...."

TINCTURE OF OPIUM...28¢

"**C**onnie, you won't believe what they have for sale in this 1897 Sears Roebuck catalog!" Don said.

"Like what?"

"Well, for 28¢ you get a four-ounce bottle of laudanum (tincture of opium), then for only $8.00 they'll sell you a dozen bottles of 'Cure For The Opium and Morphia Habit'! If you're not interested in drug addiction, you can choose from 770 pages of everything from chamber pots to a collection of over 220 rifles and handguns. They even offer a 'Princess Bust Developer' complete with a bottle of 'Bust Expander' and a jar of 'Bust Food'; all three for only $1.46!"

"Is that really in the catalog? What on earth are you reading anyway?"

"This is a hardbound 786-page copy of the *1897 Sears Roebuck Catalogue*, edited by Fred L. Israel, a professor of American History at City College of New York, and published by Chelsea House in New York City. It is rated at the top of the list for an authentic look back into the 1800s."

"You'd better stick to your insurance research."

"I am sticking to it. I thought these examples of their previous behavior might indicate what launched Sears into the insurance business."

"Does it?" Connie asked.

"Well, they offer 'Dr. Chaise's Nerve and Brain Pills' for only 60¢ per box. Six boxes are positively guaranteed to cure any disease for which they are intended."

58

"And for what diseases are they intended?"

"It says here they will cure you if you feel generally miserable or suffer with a 'thousand-and-one indescribable bad feelings, both mental and physical, among them low spirits, nervousness, weariness, lifelessness, feeling of fullness, specks floating before the eyes, gurgling or rumbling sensations in the bowels, cold feet, pain around the loins, a constant feeling of dread as if something awful was going to happen....'"

"OK, that'll be enough."

"It says these pills 'cannot be equaled by any other medicine as a cure for impotence, spermatorrhoea, night sweats, emissions, weakness of both brain and body arising from excesses and abuses of any kind. They make the weak and timid young man strong and bold again and they will give youthful vigor and a new lease on life to the old.'"

"I'll bet they kept the ingredients a secret."

"This same 'Nerve and Brain Pill' ad wants to make one thing perfectly clear, it warns you to 'Beware Of Quack Doctors who advertise to scare men into paying money for remedies which have no merit. Full and explicit directions are enclosed with every box.'"

"I don't think I want to hear any more about it."

"They offer a newly discovered cure from Australia for heart trouble — fifty doses for 50¢ or one hundred doses for 75¢. The advertisement is headed 'Dropped Dead.' It says every fourth person has a weak or diseased heart."

"That makes you wonder why they went into the life insurance business," Connie commented.

"They were probably drinking some of their own merchandise. They offer 'Peruvian Wine of Coca' for 95¢ per bottle or $10 per dozen. The ad says to always keep a bottle of 'Peruvian Wine of Coca' near you if you wish to accomplish double the amount of work or have to undergo an unusual amount of hardship... Its sustaining powers are wonderful."

"Enough! I thought I asked you to stop reading that stuff. I don't want to hear any more."

"Sure you do. This tells what Sears sold before they discovered insurance was more profitable than cheap laudanum or expensive addiction cures or even Wine of Coca. Catalog shoppers can choose from all kinds of stuff: 'Dr. Rose's Obesity Powders' help to avoid fatty degeneration of the heart and sudden death and can be purchased for only 88¢ per box. 'Dr. Rose's Arsenic Complexion Wafers' are 40¢ per small box. 'Pasteur's Microbe Destroyer' is 95¢ per half-gallon. 'Worm Syrup' only 20¢ per bottle; 'Worm Cakes,' 20¢ per dozen. 'German Stop Drinking Liquor Cure,' 24 doses for 50¢ and guaranteed to destroy all desire for liquor. Instant relief and a permanent cure for asthma is guaranteed with 'Doctor Allen's Asthma Cure' — a full-size box containing three of the 50¢ sizes is only one dollar! I'll bet your lung specialist hasn't heard about that wonder drug," said Don.

"I'll bet the federal government hadn't heard about it either," Connie quipped.

"There was no FDA in those days, just as there is no effective federal regulation of insurance today. That's why they got away with advertising ripoffs like 'An Invigorating Drink That Produces Gentle Stimulation' and is also a 'Blood Purifier.'"

"What kind of drink purifies your blood?"

"Root beer... and one 12¢ bottle makes five gallons."

"That should keep your red and white corpuscles squeaky clean!"

"Here's another medical miracle," said Don, "an 'Electric Ring for Rheumatism' for 85¢. It says all others are imitations without any curative properties."

"All right, Donald T. Easymark, that's enough for today."

"That may be enough about exotic medicine, but let me tell you about Sears' struggle for profit according to the April 1982 *Savvy* Magazine."

"Briefly, please."

"Briefly, Sears purchased Coldwell Banker, a national real estate brokerage, for $179 million and Dean Witter Reynolds, a national securities brokerage, for $607 million. It seems they felt the need for more profit."

"Doesn't Allstate make a profit?"

"Does it rain in Seattle? Do bears poop in the woods? According to *Savvy*, in 1980, Sears' merchandise group accounted for 74 percent of sales and 29 percent of earnings. Allstate, 24 percent of sales and 64 percent of earnings! What do you say to that?"

"What can I say? Evidently Allstate policyholders have only one chopstick in the chow mein."

"You're in good hands... Trust us... to make it work... for you."

ACTUARIAL PICTOGRAPHS

Don marveled at the mathematics in the 466-page *Staff Report to the Federal Trade Commission on Life Insurance Cost Disclosure*. He passed it to Connie.

"Please read these two pages and tell me what they say."

The Interest Adjusted Surrender Index: Biased Against Term Insurance — Why It Should Not Be Used to Compare Dissimilar Policies

While the NAIC Buyer's Guide advises that the IAC index should not be used to compare "dissimilar" policies, it is nowhere explained why one should not, nor is it said whether the index is biased in such comparisons and, if so, which way. Using the equivalent whole life and term policies we have developed here, we show that a straightforward comparison of interest-adjusted surrender costs is strongly and always biased against term insurance.

The observed similarity in cost between term and whole life policies in such publications as the *New York State Shopper's Guide* should not be taken as an indication that the two types cost about the same.

Proof:

$$_t\text{IAC}_x = \dfrac{{}^t\Sigma\ {}_sP_x\,(1+r)^{t-s+1} - {}_t\text{CV}_x}{\overset{..}{s_{\overline{n}|}}i}$$
$$\phantom{_t\text{IAC}_x = }{\scriptstyle s=1}$$

But

$$_t\text{CV}_x = {}_{t+1}E_x{}^1\left(\sum_{s=1}^{t}(P_x - \text{TR}_{x+s})\cdot {}_sE_x\right)$$

(See Appendix II for a derivation of this equation.)

For a whole life policy, $_sP_x = P_x$, that is, the premium is level. For term policies, $_sP_x = \text{TR}_{x+s}$ and $_t\text{CV}_x = 0$. Subtract the whole life interest adjusted cost from the term cost.

$$\dfrac{1/}{s_{\overline{n7}|}i}\cdot\left[{}^t\underset{S=1}{\Sigma}\,\text{TR}_{x+s}\,(1+r)^{t-s+1} - {}^t\underset{s=1}{\Sigma}P_x\,(1+r)^{t-S+1} + {}_t\text{CV}_x\right]$$

rearranging and substituting for $_t\text{CV}_x$ from the equation above, we have [within the brackets].

$$\left[\dfrac{{}^t\underset{S=1}{\Sigma}(P_x - \text{TR}_{x+s})\cdot {}_sE_x - {}^t\underset{}{\Sigma}(P_x - \text{TR}_{x+s})\,(1+\pi)^{t-s+1}}{{}_{t+1}E_x}\right]$$

or

$$\underset{S=1}{\overset{t}{\Sigma}}\dfrac{(P_x - \text{TR}_{x+s})\,({}_sE_x - (1+r)^{t-s+1})}{{}_{t+1}E_x}$$

But

$$\dfrac{{}_sE_x}{{}_{t+1}E_x} = \dfrac{(1+r)^{-S}}{(1+r)^{-(t+1)}}\dfrac{1_{x+s}}{1_{x+t+1}} = (1+r)^{t-S+1}\dfrac{1_{x+s}}{1_{x+t+1}}$$

So the term in brackets now becomes

$$\left[{}^{t}\sum_{s=1} (P_x - TR_{x+s}) \cdot (1+r)^{t-S+1} \qquad \left(\frac{1_{x+s}}{1_{x+t+1}} -1 \right) \right]$$

Since $s < t + 1$ for all $s = 1, 2, t$, $1_{x+t} > 1_{x+t=1}$ and the last term in parenthesis will be positive in every term. Since initially, and then for long periods of time (15 to 20 years), the differences between P_x and TR_{x+s} are positive, the whole expression will be positive. Thus the comparison (falsely!) suggests that whole life is less costly than term — when they are constructed to be exactly equivalent.

Connie handed the report back. "Damn! Unless you're an Einstein, that's hard-core hieroglyphics. I'll bet it was a headache to the FTC."

Don said, "This is the type of stuff that convinces the peasants in the countryside not to try to understand insurance because it involves too much analytical calculus."

"My only comment on that, Mr. Easymark, is *no comment!*"

$0 + $23.67 = $20.90
(Does Not Compute)

In the following letter, names, addresses and policy numbers are fictional but text and dollar amounts are factual:

```
Mr. Arnie Flugelman
12 Sucker's Grove,
Malfunction Junction, CA 99999

RE: Policy Number 60233769435WJ2833174A

Dear Mr. Flugelman:
```

This policy lapsed for nonpayment of the premium due on October 27, 1984. You can still apply for reinstatement of this policy by completing the enclosed reinstatement application form and returning it with $426.25 to pay the premiums to March 27, 1985.

Your policy provides that in the event of lapse, the cash value and any dividends, minus any loan, will be used to purchase paid-up life insurance. As the value of this paid up life insurance is only $0, we are instead enclosing a check for this value plus the accumulated value of the annuity rider of $23.67 for a total surrender amount of $20.90.

If you want to reinstate your policy,
please return the reinstatement application,
the surrender check and the premiums needed
to pay the policy to a current date. If you
have any questions, please write c/o Policy
Accounting.

                    Non-Forfeiture Processing Section
                    Policy Benefits

JT:dat

bc: Shafter, Judas & Sly., L205/Thomas A.
Judas, OA94 — To aid you in the conservation
of this policy, we are mailing you this
notice five working days prior to the mailing
of the original and the check to the
policyholder.

Don handed the letter to Connie. "I'll bet Arnie Flugelman
is still trying to untangle that one. See how many examples of
deception and meaningless insurancese you can find — and
don't lose your temper because you know how you are when
you're mad."

MALPRACTICE
(By Whom?)

"**C**onnie," Don said, "do you mind if I bellyache a little about medical malpractice insurance ripoffs?"

"Why? You're not a doctor."

"Maybe not, but I'm sure as hell a patient!"

"Well, if you're going to grouse, keep it brief."

"All right, I'll keep it brief. In 1974 the Dow Jones average dropped from over 1,000 to 607. Many insurance companies stood to lose their collective keisters! Company investment departments panicked. Money was needed to cover their crapshoot on Wall Street, so they got it the old fashioned way — by trickery. With no mention of the stock market fizzle, malpractice premiums were raised sky-high, accompanied by a torrent of propaganda about 'underwriting losses.' The companies bilked money indirectly out of medical patients who were forced to pay the doctors and hospitals which in turn were stuck with high malpractice premiums that can best be described as obscene."

"Obscene?"

"Obscenely obscene. For example, almost overnight they hit a teaching hospital with an increase from $245,000 to $1,500,000."

"But that's only one teaching hospital. Maybe the students didn't do their homework."

"Student foul-ups weren't the problem." Don held up the

"*Because the pesky companies charge so much,
your 1,000% malpractice increase comes to $22,000
and the hospital's totals $1,800,000.*"

"*Because the pesky doctors charge so much, your health
insurance premium is now $2,375 and your
deductible is raised to $500.*"

book he had been reading. "According to this, they raised rates to all hospitals nationwide in the same year. They raised rates from $64,000 to $500,000 for a Buffalo hospital, and from $40,000 to over $558,000 for a New York hospital. A Long Beach, California, hospital rate went from $340,000 to $850,000 — a measly half a million extra."

"According to the almanac, there are about 7,000 hospitals in this country," said Connie. "That should pretty well take care of their losses on Wall Street."

"Evidently it didn't," Don replied, "because they were equally brutal to about half a million doctors from coast to coast."

"What do you mean by brutal?"

"I mean physicians were overcharged unmercifully! Some new doctors were charged over $20,000 just to open a practice. Surgeons were extreme examples. According to John Guinther in his book *The Malpractitioners*, New York orthopedic surgeons might have to perform operations three or four months a year before producing income for themselves and not for the insurance company."

"That has to be the ultimate outrage!"

"Unfortunately, it isn't."

"Why not?"

"Because the ultimate outrage is the audacity of the health insurers in climbing aboard the gravy train along with the malpractice insurers and demanding astronomical rate increases, declaring that 'medical costs are out of control'!"

"Covering up their Wall Street fiasco by complaining of fake underwriting losses certainly mushroomed into a lucrative bit of extortion for the protection merchants," Connie added.

In January 1985, the "MacNeil/Lehrer News Hour" discussed the malpractice insurance problem. A past president of the Association of Trial Lawyers of America who specialized in medical malpractice cases, reported that over the five-year period ending in December 1983, more than $7 billion in premiums and about $1.7 billion in investment income was taken in, while $1.4 billion was paid in benefits. More than

President of malpractice insurance company that raised rates 1,000% requests treatment for common cold.

$8.7 billion was taken in while only $1.4 billion was paid in benefits.

That means they charged $7.3 billion for paying out $1.4 billion in benefits — and they call big government inefficient!

"Insurers have an alibi for everything," Don said. "They insist those billions of dollars are needed in their untaxed reserve funds for possible liability claims that might be filed sometime in the future. They call it a 'long tail syndrome.'"

"It sounds like a long tail all right," Connie quipped, "spelled t-a-l-e!"

In early 1985 the California legislature, like a well-trained drill team, obediently passed an insurance-sponsored law

"Of course I know it's the first day of spring! It's also the first day this year I haven't had to give my entire earnings to the malpractice insurance company for this year's policy!"
"Congratulations, doctor, now you can go to work for the IRS."

limiting medical malpractice damage awards in the courts.

One public reaction was a protest by about one hundred people, some in wheelchairs, demonstrating in front of the State Office Building in Los Angeles. Among the demonstrators was a pitiful example of poetic justice, a Long Beach insurance broker whose one healthy kidney had been removed by mistake. A superior court jury awarded him over $5 million in malpractice damages, but a judge reduced that settlement to a meager $286,000 to comply with the new California law!

"I'm in desperate straits," said the 64-year-old victim. "I'm extremely disappointed that I can't be compensated for this mistake."

When insurance money talks, lawmakers listen!

"I'm sorry, Mac, I can't let you picket with that sign. You'll
have to change that offensive word!"

"That's better, Mac. Have a nice day."

MEDIGAP SWINDLES
(Are Alive And Well)

Congress has been told in the clearest possible language how dishonest insurance companies fleece the elderly in *Abuses In The Sale Of Health Insurance To The Elderly In Supplementation Of Medicare — A National Scandal.* This is a 444-page report on a staff study by the Select Committee On Aging, U.S. House Of Representatives, 11/28/78. Comm. Pub. No. 95-160, U.S. Government Printing office, Washington D.C. It contains sworn testimony and statistics describing literally hundreds of insurance swindles.

The summary of the study, originally requested by Rep. Claude Pepper of Florida, ends as follows:

> The unvarnished truth is that while these companies talk in terms of the best interests of the elderly, they are in reality conspiring to rob them of their meager dollars. The elderly who sought to buy hope, health, and security are left with empty pockets, anger, and further disillusionment. That these practices have gone unnoticed for the past several years is a national scandal only slightly less in magnitude than the schemes of the avaricious companies and their greedy agents.

> Hon. Mario Biaggi, congressman from New York, com-

HONESTY IS
THE WORST POLICY

"We must respectfully deny the medical claim for your right foot, because we found out that a doctor treated your left foot twelve years ago."

mented: "The techniques used to hoodwink helpless seniors into purchasing phony insurance policies constitute the most crass forms of fraud."

Val J. Halamandaris, Special Counsel for the Committee on Aging, stated: "In my view there is little distinction between a man who goes into the home of senior citizens with a gun and takes their money and a man who comes into the house on the pretext of providing a valuable service, that is, selling insurance, who in effect, does the same thing, robs the senior citizen of his money. The distinction lies only in the technical ability of the law to define the difference."

Senator Lawton Chiles of the Senate committee studying the same subject testified: "We've also had reports of companies routinely denying claims when they first came in — taking the better than even chance that the elderly policyholder will not challenge their judgment and resubmit a claim."

For those who were not paying attention, please note that the summary of this 444-page congressional staff report ends as follows:

The unvarnished truth is that while these companies talk in terms of the best interests of the elderly, they are in reality conspiring to rob them of their meager dollars. The elderly who sought to buy hope, health, and security are left with empty pockets, anger, and further disillusionment. That these practices have gone unnoticed for the past several years is a national scandal only slightly less in magnitude than the schemes of the avaricious companies and their greedy agents.

NONFICTION
(They Don't Want You To Read, Charlie)

Don and Connie moved to San Diego, California. The industry policy of selling health insurance for "everything except what ails you" left them both uninsured.

Charles Alyson Chumpworth, Jr., a family friend, interrupted a fishing trip to Baja California to visit the Easymarks in San Diego. They were living in a small house leaning up against a tree on the rear of a residential lot near the Balboa Park Zoo. It could only be described as rustic. Despite its outward appearance, it was comfortable and attractive inside and the furnishings indicated better times in the past. A sign over the kitchen door warned, "If you smoke, I'll croak!" and another in the living room cautioned, "I don't care what it is, don't smoke it here!"

Bright-eyed Charlie Chumpworth and Don Easymark had been close friends since school days when they both had been banned from the campus for a week for locking a goat in the cafeteria.

Connie greeted Charlie at the door and directed him to a small den two steps down from the floor level of the main house. Don sat in front of a word processor on the short end of a large L-shaped desk. His back was to the door. On his right was a five-drawer file cabinet. Over the desk at his left towered four shelves of books. File folders and papers were everywhere. Pictures hung at random on the walls and two small signs proclaimed the following:

I DON'T MIND IF YOU SMOKE, JUST DON'T EXHALE!

and

SEX IS BETTER THAN JOGGING BECAUSE YOU DON'T HAVE TO BUY SPECIAL SHOES.

Connie said, "Don, you have company."

He turned, saw Chumpworth and exclaimed, "Charlie! What are you doing here in the fleshpots of Southern California? Welcome to Desperation Gulch!"

"I'm on my way to Bahia de Los Angeles to do a little fishing," he replied. "How are you doing?"

"I'm a few years older and a dollar broker. I'm working on a book."

"Work is a four letter word! What kind of book are you working on?"

"Fiction based on real-life atrocities. It's about insurance ripoffs."

"You certainly should know something about that. What are all those books stacked on your desk?"

"Nonfiction books and Government Printing Office bulletins about insurance swindles."

"That's really a super-duper piece of the rock. How many do you have there?"

"I haven't counted them but they weigh well over a hundred pounds, and you can be sure the industry doesn't want you to read any of them."

"I don't bother to read that kind of stuff."

"Nobody else does either, Chumpworth. No one pays attention. That's why the industry gets away with doing as it damn well pleases."

"Are you going to recommend those books to your readers?"

"You bet I am, fearless fisherman, and in particular, I'm going to recommend *The Health Insurance Racket And How To Beat It* by John E. Gregg, a lawyer, ex-FBI agent and repentant former trainer-instructor of health insurance salesmen. It focuses attention on the cheating record of health insurance companies and pinpoints their premium-payer-be-damned attitude. It also exposes the danger of allowing these companies to have access to money intended for a proposed national health care program.

"Keep in mind," Don continued, "that there is a vast difference between national health insurance administered by private companies and a true comprehensive national health care program. The private industry would like to make the biggest insurance sale in history by underwriting 'National Health Insurance.' Lobbyists will try to force-feed private health insurance to all of us by making health insurance salesmen out of the U.S. Congress! If the lobbyists have their usual success, Congress will cooperate with insurance flim-flammery. Based on the industry's past record of bilking the public, such a congressional double-cross would be a monumental national tragedy! Any teenager can tell you there is no place for profiteering and claim-dodging in an efficient national health care program."

"I'll be sure to check that out with the next teenager I meet," said Charlie.

"It's an established historical fact that health insurance business methods are influenced by the profit they can bilk out of people's inability to pay cash for modern medical care," said Don. "They profit by bleeding billions of dollars out of our health care system annually. In 1979, they took $8.8 billion more in premiums than they paid out in claims. That kind of money is a strong incentive for larcenous overcharges and cheating at patients' expense."

"How do you know they took in $8.8 billion more than they paid out?"

"I read it in the Source Book Of Health Insurance Data, 1980-1981. Any ten-year-old knows that the $8.8 billion would be put to better use if it funded medical research and higher compensation for the medical professionals who perform the really important medical services. Under our present backward health insurance system, that $8.8 billion is handed on a silver platter to financial wheeler-dealers operating out of big city skyscrapers. Would you rather dedicated doctors or dedicated fine-print jockeys handled your medical finances?"

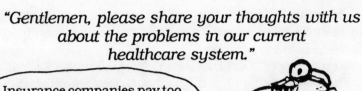

"Gentlemen, please share your thoughts with us about the problems in our current healthcare system."

Insurance companies pay too little, too slowly, with too much paperwork (if they pay at all) and malpractice premiums are breaking our backs!

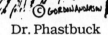

Dr. Phastbuck

Doctors and patients want too much, but we can beat them in court with trickery and fine print and we can (cackle/drool) make a bundle!

Chairman of the Board, Colossal Benefit Insurance Co.

The insurance industry put our kids through college.

Victim's Lawyer

Company Lawyer

...And it kept mine out!

"Gentlemen, what are your views on a reliable national healthcare system directed honestly by physicians... a system that protects everyone and wipes out the binge of claim dodging, unfair mass exclusions, vast overcharges and profiteering with billions of our healthcare dollars?"

NATIONAL HEALTHCARE? ARE YOU CRAZY? GOOD GOD, MAN — THAT WOULD BE UN-AMERICAN!"

"Doctors of course," said Charlie. "Fine-print jockeys could be hazardous to your health."

"The fine-print jockeys have been developing Health Maintenance Organizations (HMOs) to muscle into the health care field. HMOs can be better for patients than mail-order health insurance, but *dishonest* insurance HMOs limit choice of doctors, restrict access to specialists and kick you out of the hospital early simply to cut expenses and increase profits."

Charlie exploded. "Jesus H. Christ! What'll they think of next?"

"They'll have to think of something. They've already grabbed control of enough of the nation's money to unbalance the economy. Believe it or not, their frenzied use of tax loopholes has even changed our city skylines."

"THE HOLLOW SKYLINE," "SEE THROUGH TOWERS" AND "FINANCIAL ERECTIONS"

"**L**ook at this, Charlie," said Don. "The morning paper says Fireman's Fund suffered a $4.1-million loss in the first quarter and an $85.1-million loss in the second quarter. That's an unadulterated crock of unaccountable accounting. It says right here in the same article that the so-called 'loss' included a $191-million addition to reserves against potential insurance claims!

"*Not mentioned* is the fact that the $191 million is untaxed... *Not mentioned* is the fact that the $191 million is not just held there awaiting the opportunity to pay claims promptly and in full... *Not mentioned* is the fact that generous portions of the $191 million may be used for legal fees to defend minimizing or even total denial of such claims... *Not mentioned* is the likelihood that most of the $191 million will be used for Wall Street gambling, funding corporate takeovers and/or financing the national glut of half-vacant, tax-dodge-glass skyscrapers, better known as 'The Hollow Skyline,' 'See Through Towers' and 'Financial Erections.'"

"Egad, Easymark," Charlie replied, "now I know what is meant by Voodoo Economics!"

CRAPTOLERATION

Insurers treat victims at the top of the ladder and those at the bottom with equal contempt. William F. Buckley reports such an instance in the following column:

A friend endowed with a low threshold of what the Honorable Daniel Patrick Moynihan has called "crap-toleration" bought a house in the country and took out insurance on it 12 years ago. The seasons came and went, and he paid in his premiums promptly, never suffering fire, theft, or natural catastrophe. Then this winter, the severest in history, his pipes froze. He was covered against the contingency and the insurance company in due course issued him a check for $3,000. During the preceding years, he had paid to the company premiums amounting to about $15,000. Last week he received a communication from the company.

On hearing the description of it I concluded that my friend and I must be insured by the same company. It struck me as inconceivable that two companies in America would be so practiced in the brutal arts. It turns out that there are two companies, not one. And for all I know, the communication we both received is standard in the business. It goes something like this, a form letter with the italicized passages typed in:

Re *John M. Jones*, Policy no. *345 786 892*.
You are hereby notified that your policy will
be discontinued effective: *May 12, 1978*.
Reason: Failure to pay premium ___ Failure to
provide requested information ___ Medical ___
Other: *X prior claims*.

There is a printed signature of sorts, and that is the
end of the communication. Now these are the same
gentlemen who, when they write you a letter soliciting
your business, use a voice described by George Orwell,
referring to BBC broadcasters, as "genteel and
throaty." When they come to your house, they are a
combination of Florence Nightingale, Edward Bennett
Williams, the Archangel Gabriel, and the local cop on
the beat. They will look after you. Do not fear the
future: Put your faith in the Amalgamated Insurance
Company of America, and go gently to your destiny.

What they don't tell you is that the minute one of
those computers finds that you have staked out a claim
for what you are insured against, you are either
dropped via form letter; or your rates rise to the point
of repaying, in effect, the claim for which you have
been insured. It is not the least vexatious part of the
whole business that the insurance companies appear
to be unconcerned with the question of responsibility.
When my family suffered a theft, no insurance agent
came around to ascertain whether we had taken
reasonable precautions against theft, or whether we
were supplementing our precautions.

No one asked my friend whether he had guarded
against the possibility of his pipes freezing. There is
no time for the amenities, for a personal visit, telephone call, or letter. We have all had bad trips with the
federal bureaucracy. But the least clerk in the
government is Dale Carnegie alongside the insurance
companies.

I recall the sense of shock in late November 1972.
Richard Nixon had been re-elected by a landslide vote.

A decision had been made to clean house of appointee holdovers. Mr. Haldeman's reputation for brusqueness was greatly enhanced by the form letter he sent out. "Dear _____: Please submit your resignation to the president by November 31. Yours truly, H.R. Haldeman."

Now this letter didn't go out to stepmothers of the Nixon family, or second cousins, or political hacks, though presumably they got the same letter. It went out to hundreds of people who had been volunteering their services on presidential commissions for no pay — in discharge of the civic imperative. It made no difference to a White House inflated by inflationary victory which ultimately brought dissolution to its principals.

The symptom is identical. When someone is useful to you — to perform a civic service, to pay an insurance premium — to render sexual service — the attitude is one thing. After that, one acts like Don Giovanni toward Elvira. And look at what happened to Nixon and Don Giovanni.

Will it happen to the insurance companies? Except for one's dogmatic belief in the private sector, sometimes one almost hopes so. The telephone company in the United States has survived as a monopoly by its marvelous public manners. Now imagine a situation in which a telephone is removed from a customer because he does not run up enough long distance charges, and therefore is a statistical loss. That is the way the insurance companies, with their grand, imposing, wall-to-wall carpets and smiles in effect treat you, and my friend and I are pledged to pass along the word, and then to encourage a company, assuming one exists, whose computers have been taught table manners.

"Madame, you can't afford to be without our new
protection against over-insured motorists... and you
can't be turned down!"

7,000 BUSY SIGNALS FOR THE PEASANTRY IN FIVE DAYS!

O n May 12, 1986, the California Auditor General submitted a report on an investigation of how the State Insurance Department responds to consumers' allegations against the industry for fraud, misrepresentation, dishonesty, incompetence, or other illegal acts.

The report concluded that the Department of Insurance was not properly responsive to these complaints.

For example, in a five-day period beginning March 17, 1986, just in the Insurance Department's Los Angeles branch office, consumers received over 7,000 busy signals when calling the complaint lines!

Date	Number of Busy Signals Received
March 17, 1986 — Monday	1,842
March 18, 1986 — Tuesday	1,625
March 19, 1986 — Wednesday	1,656
March 20, 1986 — Thursday	990*
March 21, 1986 — Friday	896*
Total	7,009

*Pacific Bell's data for these days were incomplete.
Source: Pacific Bell survey of phone calls to the department.

This informative sixty-four-page report spells out details of Department of Insurance failure to properly settle consumer complaints. Copies of Auditor General reports are available for $2.00 per copy. Reports may be obtained by contacting:

Office of the Auditor General
660 J Street, Suite 300
Sacramento, CA 95814
(916) 445-0255

Permission is granted to reproduce reports.

Social problem

EASYMARK'S CONCLUSION
(4,917,080 Isolated Instances
Are Too Many!)

Deception and denial of legitimate benefits too often result in long lasting personal tragedy for victims.

Insurance buyers must keep their guard up to determine how well they are covered, if at all. Unfortunately, few policyholders are able to make this determination and too often are unable to collect at claims time. Policies are usually riddled with exceptions and enough legalistic double-talk to bewilder a Supreme Court justice.

Historically, the downfall of great nations has been caused by rotting from within. With this fact in mind, it is sad to note that our Congress and state legislatures seem ineffective against the political and financial clout of the private insurance industry.

Corrupting the free enterprise system by fleecing the populace continues with the full knowledge and approval of top insurance executives. They work shoulder to shoulder with actuaries, high-powered marketing bosses, claim supervisors and politicians. Things would change if the responsible individuals were faced with the prospect of some "hard time in the slammer" instead of being coddled and tolerated.

A glut of loosely-worded insurance legislation exists

"Don't be alarmed, folks, this is just an isolated instance."

nationwide. The California Insurance Code, for example, prohibits "knowingly committing or performing with such frequency as to indicate a general business practice any of the following unfair claims practices...." That loophole is followed by a list of common, everyday ripoffs and claim dodges.

The Idaho Department of Insurance stated in a letter that the industry "opposes restrictive legislation" and does not want to be held accountable unless it is first shown that the insurer's conduct is a "usual business practice" and not "just an isolated instance." Most offending companies classify atrocities as "isolated instances."

Such ludicrous logic means that the bank robber who has made hundreds of legitimate withdrawals should not be held accountable because he only shot a teller once — just an isolated instance. It means that the mugger who steals the little old lady's purse should not be held accountable because he has allowed thousands of little old ladies over the years to keep their purses.

Insurance companies tend to ignore the fact that "isolated instances" often cause extreme and lasting hardship for the victims.

Millions of people are cheated annually. The California Insurance Commissioner's office acknowledged receiving over 20,000 complaints in one year. In 1977 the New York Commissioner admitted to 57,000 complaints and the Florida Commissioner, 34,000.

Offending companies alibi that those thousands of complaints are not all valid. It is clear, however, that all complaining victims were cheated or deceived to a point where they believed the complaints were warranted. Even the most gullible victim knows there is nothing to be gained by making an unwarranted complaint, only to have it stashed away by some bored clerk in the insurance commissioner's office while the insurance company smugly pockets the money.

According to a Congressional Committee Staff Study, insurance commissioners of thirty-seven states and the District of Columbia admitted to receiving 366,375 complaints in one year, an average of 9,641 per state.

GORDON ANDERSON

"Don't worry, Ma'am, I don't commit or perform purse snatching with such frequency as to indicate a general business practice."

Assuming the 9,641 average also applies to the thirteen nonreporting states, there would be an additional 125,333 complaints for a total of 491,708.

One state insurance commissioner estimated that only one out of ten cheated victims files a formal complaint. This means (according to a lunch box actuarial estimate by Don Easymark) that we have 4,917,080 potential white collar insurance crimes each year in fifty states and the District of Columbia — 4,917,080 isolated instances!

Connie Easymark read through the manuscript of Don's book. She said, "Don, why haven't you given the insurance industry's side of the story?"

"Because," Don replied, "the industry spends millions of policyholders' dollars advertising and bragging about what 'good guys' they are and I couldn't add anything to that! Besides, that's not what the book is about. I wrote about the scourge of insurance ripoffs as they appear to me, then simply made reference to books by experts who describe the swindles better than I can."

"Then why don't you offer some solution to the problem?"

"Because the solution is too complicated for us peasants. The solution is our lawmakers' responsibility. The problem is, they seem to just sit there and introduce legislation written for them by industry lawyers. The lobbyists who tout that stuff should be locked deep in some capitol dungeon while lawmakers enact corrective laws with sharp teeth and no loopholes."

"That would be about as popular with the industry bosses as punitive damages for bad faith."

"Maybe so, but it would be as popular as strawberry shortcake with policyholders and registered voters who far outnumber industry bosses! Until lawmakers do the job they were elected to do, the best protection for everyone is to use caution and investigate the consequences before giving a single dime to any protection merchants, mortgage loan sharks or insurance salesmen masquerading as financial 'advisers.'"

In case the Insurance Information Institute and/or the gang at the Colossal Benefit Insurance Company should take offense at his book, Don was ready with a prepared response:

Gentlemen, this book is about the intolerable aspects of private insurance as viewed by a victim. No apology need be given for its harsh tone. This is just how an unsophisticated layman sees the rotten side of your business. It is the only book I've ever put together, so don't be concerned... It's just an isolated instance!

Don Easymark put down the evening paper to answer the persistent ring of the doorbell. As he arose, his old spinal injury sent a shot of pain down his left leg to his foot. He limped to the door.

"Good evening, Mr. Easymark. My name is Sam Sly. You were recommended to me by good old Tom Judas down at the office. Tom said you were an astute businessman and would welcome the profits from this amazing new investment opportunity tailored especially for you. It gives you a large retirement income and a $100,000 group life insurance policy that even has cash value! May I come in......?"

Part II

A Select Bibliography

Over One Hundred Pounds Of Reference Books

Rational, Fact-Filled Reading To Convince The

Human Race It Is Being Swindled

And That All Is Not Sweetness And Light

In The Private Insurance Industry!

"Don't try to list them all, life is too short!"

BOOKS THEY'D RATHER YOU DIDN'T READ
(Read Them Anyway, If You Can Find Copies Before They Disappear)

BEAT THE BASTARDS
IN COURT
(Ready For The Plaintiff)

Before presenting a major list of books critical of insurance thievery, special attention must be directed to the 338-page book by Melvin Belli published in 1956 and titled *Ready for the Plaintiff.*

Melvin Belli is an attorney who sees through the insurance rackets and is not afraid to fight them in court. He exposes them in seminars and publicizes them in print. This book was published over thirty years ago; nonetheless, the atrocities described are still with us in sophisticated and computerized form.

Insurance companies are professional defendants. Because they expect to be sued, they lubricate lawmakers and maintain armies of crafty and skilled defense attorneys. When victims are forced into court to collect legitimate benefits or settlements, the companies are ready and waiting. Belli describes the victim's plight and reports on unpublished details of the court battles.

The following excerpt is typical of the thought-provoking occurrences reported in this book:

There is another story, about a lawyer whose plaintiff had a broken leg. The break had occurred, said the plaintiff, while he was a passenger on a city bus. A negligent driver had stopped the vehicle so precipitously that claimant was thrown to the floor.

The case went to a jury trial. However, during vigorous cross-examination by the defense attorney, something was said that aroused the suspicions of the plaintiff's lawyer. At recess he got his client into a quiet corner and questioned him very, very closely. To his chagrin, the client brushed off the questions with a blatant, spine-chilling exclamation. "I was never on that bus at all! I assumed you knew that all the time."

White and shaken, plaintiff's lawyer went looking for the lawyer for the defendant bus company. Still too overcome to talk at length, he simply asked opposing counsel to accompany him to the judge's chambers. There he took a deep breath and began, "Your Honor, there's something I'd like to say about my plaintiff. I want to tell you that..."

But before he could finish, defendant lawyer interrupted. "Now just a minute, counsel," he expostulated. "If there's anything in the way of new evidence, I would prefer to have the jury hear it in open court. Our insurance company has just found four witnesses who saw your plaintiff on that bus and each one of them is ready to swear that he was dead drunk at the time of the accident. We'll show, by unimpeachable evidence, that the accident was absolutely his fault!"

PAYMENT REFUSED

By *William M. Shernoff, attorney and nationally known leader in insurance bad faith litigation. Richardson & Steirman, Inc., 1986.*

How to fight back against the welter of phony and dishonest insurance practices. Here are practical legal tips, including how to handle claim problems, from a nationally prominent attorney for victims.

Readers will be fascinated by reports on actual court cases with a number of details published for the first time.

This is a long overdue report on how courts have awarded damages for claims swindles against Mutual of Omaha, AARP-sanctioned Colonial Penn Franklin, Blue Cross, Commercial Bankers, Prudential and Metropolitan.

The medical profession will be interested in how Shernoff negotiated a settlement with an estimated value of between $50 million and $61 million for return of excess medical malpractice premiums pocketed by Travelers Insurance company when Travelers had originally refused to return a single dime!

Whether cheating insurers like it or not, this book is available in bookstores or may be ordered at:

PAYMENT REFUSED
976 W. Foothill Boulevard,
Claremont, CA 91711

MR. BAD-WRENCH

By *Arthur P. Glickman, former reporter for the* Wall Street Journal *and the* Pittsburgh Press, *author of* The Great American Auto Repair Robbery. *Wideview Books, 1981.*

Here is a 447-page manual on how to survive the $20 billion-a-year auto repair ripoff.

Part I, "Mr. Bad-Wrench Has You By The Ball Joints," includes a close look at the relationship between auto insurance companies and auto body shops. It explains why body shops agree to shoddy repairs to comply with standards imposed by adjusters and how they are forced to sell their souls to the "bad hands people."

A disturbing number of swindles are fully documented, such as the case of a New York man who totalled his car while driving to work. For six years he had been paying $60 per year for collision insurance without a claim. Even though comparable cars sold for $650, the Travellers Indemnity adjuster insisted the car was worth only $272 and that, less his $200 deductible, would entitle him to a settlement of just $72!

Glickson cites thieving tricks galore and extends a warning that complaining to the State Insurance Commissioner is often futile because many commissioners come from the insurance industry and plan to go back when their term of office is over.

Mr. Bad-Wrench is a valuable one-volume library on problems all car owners face.

WHAT'S WRONG WITH YOUR LIFE INSURANCE
By Norman F. Dacey, head of his own firm of financial consultants and trustees, author of over 100 articles on estate planning and sought-after lecturer. Macmillan, 1963.

More than 400 pages outline atrocities by life insurance companies.

Thirty-seven pages describe sales methods used to lure buyers into financial quicksand and 408 pages (of facts) describe that quicksand.

Billions of dollars are drained away from the public in the guise of "protection." Between 1940 and 1960 the industry paid out $89 billion in benefits and all they asked for doing it was $260 billion. During these same twenty years, they "mislaid" $14 billion still unaccounted for!

What's Wrong With Your Life Insurance is one of the most informative books on life insurance abuses — what your life insurance agent doesn't tell you.

THE MORTALITY MERCHANTS
The Legalized Racket Of Life Insurance And What You Can Do About It
By G. Scott Reynolds, investment counselor, head of Reynolds & Company, S.E.C. Registered Broker and general agent for several life insurance companies. D. McKay Co., 1968.

A report on the hodgepodge of life insurance schemes

deliberately designed to drain the nation's pocketbook. This excellent book is best described by a quote from its preface:

The following pages will not concern themselves with savings, college funds, investments, tax matters, retirement or any of the other fields of family finance into which life insurance men so insistently meddle — other than to document the industry's own misleading, if not fraudulent excursions into these areas.

The enormous and needless complexities of life insurance exist for a single purpose — to keep the buyer off balance and in a state of confusion. The inadequacy of regulation of the industry at the state level and the almost total absence of it at the federal level, leave the public to fend for itself against the monumental abuses of life insurance.

Here are details of the financial trap into which most policyholders have fallen. This book usually can be found in public and college libraries.

PAY NOW, DIE LATER
By James Gollin, C.L.U., a Chartered Life Underwriter with a Masters degree in English from Yale University. Random House, 1966 and Penguin Paperback, 1969 (Revised).

Here is an expert's view of life insurance gimmickry, with the hard facts clearly described in Yale English. The industry has much to hide, much to be ashamed of and embarrassed by.

People entrapped in this business have given information in exchange for the author's promise not to reveal their identities.

The chapters entitled "Hell, We'll Hire Any Warm Body" and "Just Con Them a Little" describe the coldblooded exploitation of insurance agents by their own companies. These chapters are reprinted in Part III of this book.

THE STOCKHOLDER
By William Hoffman, author and former employee of the sole

owner and only stockholder of Bankers Life of Chicago, the late John D. MacArthur. Lyle Stuart, Inc., 1969.

A biography of the late billionaire John MacArthur and a report on the cheating and sharp practices involved in the rise of one of the nation's largest health insurers, Bankers Life Insurance Company of Chicago. Bankers Life paid claimants only 1 percent of premium revenue for two consecutive years. When asked about this outrage, MacArthur said, "It must have been a good year, these things happen, you know, times when nobody gets sick."

A classic MacArthur remark was: "Sue? Go ahead. I've got thirty-five hundred lawsuits now. Yours will make thirty-five hundred and one."

A former speaker of the Alabama House of Representatives testifying before a House judiciary committee referred to Bankers as "a vicious racket that drains more dollars out of the pockets of rural families than almost anything else I know of. It's legal theft — that's what it amounts to!"

Here is a fascinating insight into the evil genius behind the billion dollar corporate thievery of a giant health insurer.

A COMPENDIUM OF BUNK (HOW TO SPOT A CON ARTIST)
By Mary Carey and George Sherman. Charles C. Thomas, 1976.

This is a handbook for fraud investigators, bankers and other custodians of the public trust. It explores a wide range of fraud practiced by confidence men and includes six pages on insurance sharpies. These two sentences alone are worth the price of the book:

> The most common swindle is the insurance policy which is so riddled with exceptions and so legalistic in its language that it would take a Ph.D. to figure out how the policyholder is covered, if at all. Very few layman can read insurance policies, and fewer still will be able to make an insurer who writes this kind of policy pay off when the need arises.

In 1985 this book was still available from Charles C. Thomas Publishing, 301-327 East Lawrence Ave., Springfield, Illinois.

THE GREAT WALL STREET SCANDAL
Inside Equity Funding
By Raymond Dirks, a brilliant insurance securities analyst who has been a senior analyst with Bankers Trust, Goldman Sachs & Co., and is a former senior vice-president of a Wall Street research firm. Co-authored by Leonard Gross, a ranking journalist and a former senior editor of LOOK Magazine. McGraw-Hill, 1974.

The title is a misnomer. A first-hand report by the courageous analyst who risked his career to expose this monumental fraud, the Equity Funding swindle is more of an insurance scandal than a Wall Street scandal. This is the inside story of more than $100 million in fictitious assets; bogus insurance policies; forged death certificates; counterfeited bonds; doctored computer tapes; fraudulent records. An example of how insurance companies can defraud the public for years virtually unhampered by regulators. The reader will ask how many more companies engage in such practices.

THE IMPOSSIBLE DREAM
(Equity Funding, The Fraud Of The Century)
By Ronald L. Soble, financial reporter for the Los Angeles Times, and Robert E. Dallos, journalism professor of New York University and New York financial correspondent for the Los Angeles Times. Signet, 1975.

Another report on Equity Funding's orgy of corporate deceit. *A story of what happened once — and what, if we are not careful, can be happening all around us.* A blow-by-blow account of the fall of a financial empire illustrated with photos of principal characters and a Paul Conrad editorial cartoon.

OUTRAGEOUS MISCONDUCT
By Paul Brodeur, a staff writer for The New Yorker specializing in environmental and occupational medicine and author of The Zapping Of America. Pantheon Books, 1985.

Here is a detailed account of the problems encountered by

asbestos companies in settling the lawsuits filed by victims of asbestos-related diseases. Revealed are some of the stumbling blocks faced by companies in collecting from insurers who supposedly provide protection.

In addition to a documented report on claim-dodging, the chapter entitled "Getting Off The Risk" tells of an almost unbelievable cover-up by the insurance industry that might well have cost tens of thousands of lives and caused untold suffering and pain.

As far back as 1935, insurance companies were aware of the asbestos dangers revealed clearly in their own actuarial statistics, their own doctors' reports and their own workman's compensation claims.

Instead of sounding the alarm publicly and saving lives, rates were quietly increased to compensate for the risks. During the following half-century, disease, disability and death from asbestos increased and the industry collected astronomical amounts in premium and investment revenue while silently settling claims out of bloated reserves with a minimum of publicity.

The reader will have reason to question whether a private industry with such a dismal record should be allowed to participate in a national health care program.

JUDGMENT
A Case Of Medical Malpractice
By Gail Kessler, Ph.D., a magazine writer with a doctorate in English from Columbia University. Mason/Charter, 1976.

An examination of the medical, legal, psychological, ethical and personal aspects of a malpractice lawsuit on behalf of a female paraplegic confined for life to a wheelchair. Included is a report on the insurance company's attempt to avoid paying fair compensation by offering a "gift" of $10,000 for a release... then $60,000... then $150,000... then $200,000, until finally a jury awarded her $404,000, $394,000 more than the original "gift" offer.

This well-researched book quotes a Department of Health, Education & Welfare report that *plaintiffs' lawyers receive only 10¢ to 15¢ of the malpractice dollar, while 40¢ goes to defense lawyers who defend the persistent claim-dodging of insurance companies!*

Readers will wonder why many of our legislators sit back and wink at the brazen impropriety of the daily insurance swindles.

THE INVISIBLE BANKERS
(Everything The Insurance Industry Never Wanted You To Know)
By Andrew Tobias, respected financial writer, Harvard MBA and author of several books. Linden Press/Simon & Schuster, 1982.

One of the best comprehensive studies of the private insurance industry, here is an educational and entertaining portrayal of the industry's horns along with its halos.

This affordable book, available in both paperback and hardcover, conceivably could save the purchaser hundreds or even thousands of times the purchase price.

The author states, "I have never personally suffered at the hands of an insurance company." Could it be that Harvard MBAs have found a way to tolerate obscene overcharges?

THE LIFE INSURANCE CONSPIRACY
Formerly Holmes And Watson Solve The Almost Perfect Crime — Life Insurance
By Peter Speilmann and Aaron Zelman, with contributions by Dean Sharp, former counsel and investigator for the U.S. Senate Judiciary Committee's Antitrust and Monopoly Subcommittee Hearings on Life Insurance. Simon & Schuster, 1979.

Dean Sharp comments on "cash value" life insurance in the introduction:

Today, as an independent life insurance broker — free to sell any kind of policy that best suits a consumer — as well as a practicing lawyer, I am made aware constantly of the cash-value life insurance "racket."

109

And I am convinced it is a racket, a scam not unlike the "sting" sort of confidence game whereby the agent leads the consumer to believe he will get "something for nothing" — that his insurance will "cost him nothing in the long run." As in any confidence game, greed and ignorance propel the buyer into the deal. He must realize that if the insurance costs him nothing, surely somebody, somehow, must be paying for it. But so long as the buyer thinks somebody else is the sucker, he will sign up now, while the offer holds. Only too late, if ever, does the buyer discover that he, himself, has been the sucker.

Speilmann and Zelman describe the swindles in factual and easily understood language.

Abuses by the industry go back over a hundred years and are common enough to victimize almost every family in America. What is good for the companies is not always good for insurance buyers. This excellent book will help readers to avoid future insurance problems.

THE CLAIMS GAME
Inside Secrets And Techniques Of Collecting
Insurance Claims
By Vladimir P. Chernik, a senior claims supervisor with a staff of insurance attorneys at his disposal. Sherbourne Press, 1969.

Inside information, valuable to anyone trying to get a fair settlement from an insurance company. An advisory on the slick tricks used by "claims jockeys" to deny benefits, this book will help the reader avoid being short-changed on legitimate insurance claims.

More than 200 fact-filled pages of what the insurance adjuster doesn't want you to know.

The Consumer's Guide to INSURANCE BUYING
By Vladimir P. Chernik, author of The Claims Game. Sherbourne Press, 1970.

Don't let the title fool you! This is a valuable reference and forewarning of ripoffs as well as a guide to what you should insure, how much you ought to spend and when not to bother with any insurance in the first place. A full 288 pages of valuable information by an expert.

The Consumer's Guide To INSURANCE
By Vladimir P. Chernik. Wm. H. Wise & Co., 1972.

Owning this book, a combination of two of Chernik's prior books, *Consumer's Guide To Insurance Buying* and *The Claims Game*, is like having a highly skilled insurance man working to protect your interests — not just trying to get your money.

One chapter tells why salesmen are driven to deceit and even fraud. Titles like "Million Dollar Round Table member," "C.L.U." and "C.P.C.U." may indicate a certain knowledge of insurance but should not be mistaken for a guarantee of competency or honesty.

An expert describes in 512 pages what to look *for* as well as what to look *out for*, such as the many pitfalls of auto insurance and how to avoid health insurance booby-traps.

THE GREAT AMERICAN INSURANCE HOAX
By Richard Trubo, journalist, and Richard Guarino, Attorney for the State of California. Nash Publishing, 1974.

An attorney and journalist discuss, in easily understandable terms, a broad spectrum of insurance bad faith activities such as: Americans priced out of the health insurance market; difficulty getting health insurance for the ailment most likely to run up your medical bills; disability insurance fraud; claims denied by disability insurers; damages awarded for disability victims up to $5,126,000 against cheating companies; mail-order insurance rackets; a victim's claim denied for right foot problems because insurer discovered his left foot had been treated by a doctor twelve years earlier; National Home Life denies 30,290 claims out of 78,577 in 26 months; insurance pushing by celebrities like Paul Harvey and Art Linkletter; enormous profits from the questionable practices

*"Nothing can replace your Colossal Benefits... and I must respectfully inform you it has just **replaced yours!**"*

of mail-order insurers; deceptive games of life insurers; auto insurance outrages, and much more. These are just a few of the atrocities in this 300-page book.

A revised and updated paperback edition was published by Doubleday in 1975 under the gung-ho title *Your Insurance Handbook.*

THE NORTH WILL RISE AGAIN
By Jeremy Rifkin and Randy Barber, The People's Business Commission, a Washington, D.C. educational organization. Beacon Press, 1978.

Anyone relying on a pension for retirement must read this book. A significant number of pension funds, both public and private, are administered by private insurance companies. Pension agreements, like insurance policies, are often loaded with fine print "legally" permitting the insurance company to keep your money without giving you a single dime!

One example of the plague of pension abuses is the case of the sales clerk in New York City who was laid off for a few short weeks immediately following the Christmas rush season, only to learn, when he reached sixty-five years of age, that as a result of that layoff, he had forfeited any rights to a retirement income! The cruelty of being left high and dry in the last few years of life is an unpardonable sin by any standard, a practice prohibited today by laws (riddled with loopholes).

This is a brilliant and well-researched analysis of what happens to your pension dollar.

LIFE INSURANCE COST DISCLOSURE
A Staff Report To The Federal Trade Commission
By the FTC Bureau of Consumer Protection and Bureau of Economics. U.S. Government Printing Office, 1979

This 466-page report created a wave of panic throughout the life insurance industry, which in turn unleashed the full fury of the powerful life insurance lobby against the FTC. This resulted in well-lubricated congressional sanctions prohibiting the FTC from investigating the insurance industry.

The sanctions freed the companies to continue selling millions of dollars of overpriced policies, bilking the poor and the elderly and engaging in deceptive practices without having to worry about FTC intervention.

The crippling of the FTC has destroyed the effective services of an agency created to protect the public against deceptive, misleading, unfair and illegal business practices. Consumers will suffer most.

The report recommends that life insurers be required to disclose the rate of return along with other pertinent pricing information in a simple and effective manner to insurance buyers. This requirement for simple honesty is violently opposed by insurance companies.

113

PRESCRIPTION FOR NATIONAL HEALTH INSURANCE
(A Proposal for the U.S. Based on Canadian Experience)
By Peter Fisher, newspaper and radio reporter and editor, market researcher and sales executive. North River Press, Box 241, Croton-on-Hudson, N.Y. 10520, 1972.

Read this book and you will understand the superiority of British Columbia's health care system over our own backward fiasco that allows insurance companies to pocket your hard-earned health care dollars.

British Columbia's system satisfies almost everyone concerned, including the public, the medical profession and the government. The coverage is total and the cost a tiny fraction of what U.S. policyholders would have to pay for the same benefits. In contrast to the U.S. private insurance system, there is no claim-dodging. Ninety-nine percent of the doctors participate voluntarily.

The government doesn't interfere with medical practice; doctors' paperwork has decreased 75 percent; and obscene profits for private insurers have been wiped out.

Based on hard facts and actual experience, this book shows how to set up a completely nonsocialistic national health care system far better and for far less than we are now spending — if the big insurance corporations, a few hidebound doctors and the U.S. Congress would permit it.

THE GRIM TRUTH ABOUT LIFE INSURANCE
By Ralph Hendershot, former financial editor of the New York World Telegram and Sun, *a veteran of thirty-seven years in the nation's financial center. Putnam Publishing, 1957.*

Chapter titles pretty well describe the book. For example: "Life Insurance — A Sacred Cow, With High Priced Milk"; "Do-It-Yourself Insurance and Your First Glimpse of the Three-Way Overcharge"; "Phantom Savings Accounts and Booby-Trap Cash Values"; "'Dividends' of Mutual Companies, or, How to Get Your Overcharge Back With a Smile."

If you have been hoodwinked by life insurance, the author says it is not because you're stupid, but because it has been presented to you under such sales pressure, and with such an array of calculation, that you never had a chance to learn the real facts. It's time you did.

This book clarifies how the cash value in life insurance dies with you, so you'd better get it out while you're still alive. It also reports on malpractice by insurers in the 1950s and the warnings are valid today.

Look for it in university libraries and used book stores. Hard to find but it will be worth the effort.

LIKE A THIEF IN THE NIGHT

By James B. Epperson, a veteran life insurance agent. Privately printed in 1939.

This little black hardbound book with the gold inlaid title is nearly impossible to find. It describes life insurance pitfalls as only an enlightened agent honestly can.

Here are details of company action to prevent attempts by agents to give policyholders the best value for their insurance dollar. "Twisting" is an industry-coined word for advising a client to replace overpriced policies with more fairly priced insurance — an honest practice violently opposed by the industry.

Epperson predicted in 1939 that the industry was bound to be snared in the net of public opinion. Forty-eight years later, tragic as it may seem, public opinion has not snared it yet.

HOW I GOT MY PIECE OF THE ROCK

Frank S. J. McIntosh, Editor. Privately published by Frank S.J. McIntosh, P.O. Box 468, Brevard, NC 28712, 1979.

This illustrates the magnitude of the loss to the American public from "cash value" insurance schemes, and the reason the industry controls a major part of the nation's wealth today.

Here is a highly informative publication in two parts. Part One is a transcript of a Santa Barbara, California, civil case resulting in judgments for damages totaling $160,000. The award was against Prudential Insurance Company and one of its agents for brutal and damaging harassment of an honest agent who advised clients to cancel "cash value" insurance

115

"You have the privilege of converting your G.I. term insurance to whole life insurance with cash value."

"Do I also have the privilege of converting steak and lobster to candied liverwurst and preserved turnips?"

and then purchase more and better coverage for less money. This portion of the book includes copies of correspondence between McIntosh and Prudential's legal department.

Part Two is devoted to documentation of "cash value" schemes over the past century, a true American tragedy. Observations by experts from coast to coast and testimony from congressional investigations are quoted.

Worth the price of the book is a transcript of a phone conversation between the president of a Florida financial corporation and the Florida Insurance Commissioner's office. Cassettes of this conversation clearly show how some regulatory commissions defend "cash value" scams to the detriment of policyholders.

This privately published volume will help the reader avoid old established shell games.

LIFE INSURANCE: A LEGALIZED RACKET
By Mort and E. Albert Gilbert. Marlowe Publishing Co., Philadelphia, and Farrar & Rinehart, New York, 1934 and 1936.

The circa-1936 gimmicks described here are still around today in computerized form. People buy insurance blindfolded, content to take the ballyhoo of agent and company as gospel.

This hard-to-find book reports in detail on industry malpractice in the depression of the early thirties. The wealth of the industry in 1933 was a monument to the gullibility of policyholders.

Look for it in antiquarian bookstores.

PAIN AND PROFIT
The Politics Of Malpractice
By Sylvia Law and Steven Polan, lawyers with broad experience in the health policy field. Harper & Row, 1978.

The American Medical Association estimated that nationally, the average doctor's 1975 malpractice insurance premium was $7,887.

According to the National Association of Insurance

Commissioners the national average loss per physician was $668. This looks like a charge of $7,887 to distribute $668 in benefits!

Here is one of the best objective and documented analyses of the so-called malpractice insurance "crisis" available. The 305 pages describe the parts played by patients, the medical profession, lawyers and insurers in the malpractice problem.

This major work is praised by professionals such as George A. Silver, M.D., Professor of Public Health, Yale University School of Medicine; Phillip Lee, J.D., Dir. Health Policy Program, University of California, San Francisco; Sidney Wolfe, M.D., Dir. Health Research Group, Washington, D.C.; Max W. Fine, Exec. Dir. Committee for National Health Insurance.

How valid are insurance companies' claims of excessive losses? What about the illicit love affair between the regulatory agencies and the industry they pretend to regulate? Answers are in this book.

REVOLT AGAINST REGULATION

By Michael Pertschuk, former chairman of the Federal Trade Commission and one-time Senate staff member. University of California Press, 1982.

An invaluable report from a government insider. Pertschuk headed the Federal Trade Commission during the investigation of life insurance cost disclosure. He reports on how the government is bullied by the private insurance industry.

When the FTC investigated the life insurance industry, the Senate Commerce Committee did not object *until the life insurance industry erupted in wrath.* On November 20, 1979, the Commerce Committee, by a vote of fifteen to none, adopted an amendment to the FTC Act barring the commission from ever studying insurance – a legislative prefrontal lobotomy.

Among the lobbyists was the president of both Aetna and the American Council of Life Insurance, a leader of Businessmen for Carter and friend of the president. His firm had delivered to the Senate Commerce Committee members an artful brief "establishing" the commission's illegitimacy in conducting its study of life insurance cost disclosure.

Here is a scrupulously honest report on the unholy alliance between Congress and special interest organizations.

THE GREAT AMERICAN AUTO REPAIR ROBBERY
A Ten-Billion Dollar National Swindle

By Donald A. Randall and Arthur P. Glickman. Randall was Assistant Counsel to the Senate Antitrust and Monopoly Subcommittee of the Judiciary Committee during a U.S. Senate investigation of the auto repair industry. Glickman has been a reporter for newspapers including the Wall Street Journal *and the* Pittsburgh Press. Charterhouse, 1972.

You can thank the conniving greed of private insurance companies for a substantial portion of a $10-billion national auto repair swindle.

Randall and Glickman describe the manipulation by insurance companies of cost, quality and payment for collision repair. This is an obscure insurance disservice to car owners.

The authors report in detail about insurance bullying of collision victims and auto body shops alike. The harassment of paint and body shops is a national outrage.

They warn not to expect too much when sending a complaint to the state insurance commissioner because some of these commissions may be dominated by the giant insurance companies they supposedly regulate.

A worthwhile book with valuable information for any motorist.

CANCER INSURANCE: EXPLOITING FEAR FOR PROFIT

A report (together with additional views) by the Select Committee On Aging, Ninety-Sixth Congress. Comm. Pub. No. 96-202, U.S. Government Printing Office, Washington D.C., March 25, 1980.

The most comprehensive study of cancer insurance ever undertaken. It concludes that there is good reason for concern about its limited value and the fear tactics used to market it. Almost 300 pages of findings include market conduct examinations of four major cancer insurers: American

Family, American Income, Union Fidelity and Washington National.

Countless violations of laws and regulations are listed. For example, Union Fidelity advertised a $150,000 cancer plan where it was virtually impossible for the consumer to collect benefits even approaching the policy limit. In order to collect $150,000 in full, the policyholder must have cancer diagnosed more than 120 days after policy issuance and, in the thirty-six-month period immediately after the diagnosis, be confined to a qualified hospital for a minimum period of 555 consecutive days.

Part VII of this report describes phony "trusts" set up to avoid state insurance regulation. Union Fidelity established what it calls The National Senior Citizens Group Insurance "Trust." The Nevada Insurance Commissioner wrote, "I am convinced the coverage is poor and the information supplied

"Quick, Eunice! Get the checkbook! Valley Forge Insurance Company of Chicago sent me a certificate of guaranteed acceptance in the Senior Citizens Group Insurance Trust. It looks like a municipal bond and even has a gold seal!"

the prospective insured is deceptive, misleading and less than truthful."

Union Fidelity also established the United Catholic Group Insurance "Trust," used to promote a policy to "protect Catholics against cancer." The Vermont commissioner said, "There is so much objectionable and misleading about the promotional techniques as well as the basic coverage that one doesn't know where to begin in condemning it."

Union Fidelity is not alone; it is mentioned here only as an example of the information in this report. Thirty-two other insurance companies are targeted in this 292-page federal government publication. A source of shocking facts.

HOW LIFE INSURANCE COMPANIES ROB YOU
And What You Can Do About It
By Walter S. Kenton, Jr., C.L.U., a Chartered Life Underwriter, "Million Dollar Round Table" member and insurance broker. Retired from insurance, he is now Director of Estate Planning for a college in Virginia. Random House, 1982.

The author states, "Insurance may be the most essential purchase of your life, but the only way you can get it is from a ruthless industry that brainwashes its salesmen and sends them out to take you for as much as they can get."

A truly knowledgeable insider blows the whistle on life insurance selling practices. The result is arguably the most authoritative, eye-opening, convincing exposé of this multi-billion dollar industry ever published.

Kenton says:

I'm sure there must be other experienced, successful insurance salesmen who went into this with the finest of motives and who have since realized how much they were brainwashed, that they are not serving their clients but preying on them. But they have worked themselves up to good incomes, with wives and children dependent on them — and they're trapped. They can't quit. They've got to keep on with this shoddy lifestyle, burying their better instincts, keeping the truth to themselves, putting up a big front with other agents at luncheon meetings.... Well, I was fortunate that, when I realized what I was doing, I could quit. And I did.

THE SCREWING OF THE AVERAGE MAN

By David Hapgood, an investigative reporter and writer-editor. Doubleday, 1974, and Bantam paperback, 1975.

A book that describes what you may have suspected but could never prove, revealing a broad spectrum of ripoffs to which the average person is subjected. Thirty pages are devoted to a condensed report on screwings by the experts, the insurance moguls. A sampling:

"Wordnoise" is defined as verbal fakery designed to mask reality...an example is your insurance contract and another is what your agent says when you ask him what the contract means. He spouts insurance euphemisms across the kitchen table like "If, God forbid, you should pass away...." The client doesn't understand any of the policies, which is hardly surprising, since the agent doesn't understand much about them either, other than his commission rates. The agent is not the expert, only the expert's salesman and most salesmen are, like their clients, losers in the net screwing system. The winner is not at that kitchen table.

Thoroughly enjoyable and you will be better off for reading it.

THE AVERAGE MAN FIGHTS BACK

By David Hapgood, author of The Screwing of the Average Man; *in collaboration with Richard Hall, a recent Yale graduate. Doubleday, 1977.*

This sequel to *The Screwing of the Average Man* tells of phony sales pitches, deliberate complicating of policy language, failure of regulatory systems and a college life insurance hustle that deceives and victimizes students. One chapter quotes Dean Sharp, who was in charge of insurance investigation for the U.S. Senate Antitrust and Monopoly Subcommittee for eleven years. Sharp compares premium income with the amount paid in benefits by auto insurers. For example, in 1974 $8.5 billion in premiums produced $3.6 billion in paid claims — the rest disappeared up the chimney. He notes that the states do not have the manpower to regulate the industry even if they wanted to, and tells why.

Sentry Insurance put out a simple, readable auto policy and some of the policyholders who received the policy in the mail threw it in the wastebasket, evidently assuming it must be an ad because of its clarity and simplicity.

No less than ten company names begin with "Lincoln" (even though insurance wasn't Honest Abe's game).

Here are cold facts about how insurers hit below the belt.

The Average Man Fights Back ranks with The Screwing Of The Average Man as a source of valuable information.

BUY NOW, PAY LATER

By Hillel Black, a reporter formerly with the New York Times, Associated Press and CBS. William Morrow Company, 1961.

This book is an exposé of the credit rackets, and should not be confused with Pay Now, Die Later, the classic exposé of life insurance rackets.

It deals with the explosion in debt-living through credit cards, small loans, installment purchases and bank charge plans. Much of the gimmickry involves credit insurance swindles.

In a one-year period, Texas debtors paid out $92 million for credit life, health and accident insurance. Loan sharks and insurance sharks pocketed $80 million and paid out just 14¢ on the dollar in benefits. Loan sharking and insurance are closely related. When huge sums of money are taken from the public, much of it is loaned out at exorbitant cost to the borrower, thereby pyramiding profits for the lender.

When usury laws restrict huge interest charges, loan sharks set up insurance companies and rip off borrowers with outrageously high unregulated charges for "credit insurance." In one six-month period, a loan-shark-controlled insurance company collected over $155,000 in premiums and paid out

$1,600 in claims. That is less than 1.5¢ paid out on every dollar paid in by borrowers!

This behind-the-scenes report reveals startling facts about so-called "credit insurance."

WINNING YOUR PERSONAL INJURY SUIT

By John Guinther, investigative reporter and author of The Malpractitioners *and* Moralists and Managers. *Anchor Press /Doubleday, 1980.*

This book contains important information for anyone who is filing a personal-injury lawsuit.

Leon Katz, judge, Philadelphia Court of Common Pleas and former chancellor, Philadelphia Bar Association, calls it "an accurate and eminently practical book that is must reading for anyone who has suffered an injury at the hands of another.... A candid and forthright step-by-step tour through the personal-injury legal system."

A virtual goldmine of valuable information, it will help the reader obtain every dollar due under the existing legal system. From how to find a qualified lawyer and what to do when your lawyer is a lemon to how to protect yourself when insurance gumshoes are investigating you.

The 292 pages tell how to fight back against high-powered insurance companies and their no-less-high-powered lawyers.

For readers interested in claims adjusters' ability to use techniques that spy on a litigant's every act and word, wherever he or she may be, the following seven books are recommended:

THE POLITICS OF PRIVACY

By Rule, McAdam, Stearns and Uglow. Mentor, 1980.

PRIVACY How To Protect What's Left Of It

By Robert Ellis Smith. Anchor Press/Doubleday, 1979.

THE PRIVATE SECTOR

By George O'Toole. W.W. Norton, 1978.

DOSSIER The Secret Files They Keep On You
By Aryeh Neier. Stein and Day, 1975.

THE ASSAULT ON PRIVACY
By Arthur R. Miller. Mentor, 1971.

THE INTRUDERS
By Senator Edward V. Long. Frederick A. Praeger, Publishers, 1967.

BUSINESS INTELLIGENCE AND ESPIONAGE
Richard M. Greene, Jr., Editor. Dow Jones-Irwin, Inc., 1966.

Insurance behavior after the great 1906 San Francisco earthquake and fire is mentioned in the following two books:

THE SAN FRANCISCO EARTHQUAKE
By Gordon Thomas and Max Morgan Witts. Stein and Day, 1971.

"Only six major companies — four American and two English — honored their liabilities in full, without delay, with no demands for cash discount. Forty-three American companies and sixteen foreign ones spent months, and sometimes years, fighting delaying paper battles to avoid meeting their commitments."

BIOGRAPHY OF A BUSINESS 1872–1942
By Marquis James. Bobs-Merrill, 1942.

This biography of a major insurance company reports on some of the claim-dodges practiced during the San Francisco earthquake disaster. For example, companies would be liable for fire damage only. If a house was thrown down by the 'quake and then swept by fire, insurance could not be collected.

At the time newspaper headlines read, "Seventy-one Companies Will Bunko The Policyholders — Thus Far Only Thirty-Two Insurance Concerns Make Pretense To Honesty."

THE GREAT AMERICAN MEDICINE SHOW
The Unhealthy State Of U.S. Medical Care And What Can Be Done About It
By Spencer Klaw, a freelance writer, former associate editor of Fortune *Magazine and part-time teacher at Columbia University Graduate School of Journalism. Viking Press, 1975.*

The truth about our crazy-quilt health insurance coverage and the imperfections in our non-system of health care. An intelligent, serious exposure of an American failure together with some convincing suggestions for reform.

CORPORATE POWER AND SOCIAL CHANGE
The Politics Of The Life Insurance Industry
By Karen Orren, professor of Political Science, U.C.L.A. Johns Hopkins Press, 1974.

An educated account of an industry with huge resources at its disposal and how its executives avoid accounting to stockholders, policyholders and the government on the use of this money.

Included is a description of how state legislatures are kept under control: *lawmakers incur obligations through accept-ance of services as surely as through cash payoffs.*

HOT WAR ON THE CONSUMER
Edited by David Sanford. Pitman/New Republic, 1969.

A collection of articles from the *New Republic* including articles by Gilbert Friedman and James Ridgeway.

U.S. Senate hearings conducted by the late Sen. Phillip Hart reveal how the ten largest stock property and casualty companies reported an underwriting loss of $273 million in 1967, but when their accounting methods were changed to the type usually accepted by corporations the so-called "loss" turned into a profit of $55 million! In addition to the $55 million, their income from investing policyholder premiums and reserves was $1.7 billion!

Included are discussions of auto insurance problems;

credit insurance abuses; refusal to write surety bonds for minorities; sleight-of-hand accounting; "redlining"; and other problems that continue year after year in spite of the pretense at regulation.

SUPER THREATS
How To Sound Like A Lawyer And Get Your Rights On Your Own
By John M. Striker and Andrew O. Shapiro, both lawyers. Rawson Associates, 1977.

"Insurance companies are in business primarily to take in premiums, not to pay claims.... When it comes to honoring the terms of a policy, many insurance companies play Ping-Pong, batting you back and forth between the home office and the local claims office, while you are required to complete and fill out extensive questionnaires and proof of loss forms."

This book includes sample letters, petitions and legal language and cases to help you get your rights on your own.

If a good lawyer is not available to you, read this book. In fact, read it anyway, you will be glad you did.

MELVIN BELLI: MY LIFE ON TRIAL
By Melvin Belli with Robert Blair Kaiser, a journalist. William Morrow Co., 1976.

An autobiography of the colorful San Francisco attorney who has salvaged millions of dollars for victims of claim-dodging insurers.

Belli says, "Insurance company executives seemed to forget they were holding other people's money in trust. They had come to regard the money as theirs and they would be damned if they'd give it up without a struggle, or even account for it. They still won't...and don't."

Here is a truly fascinating book about a lawyer who resents being called an ambulance chaser — he would rather be there before the ambulance arrives!

THE FINEST JUDGES MONEY CAN BUY
And Other Forms Of Judicial Pollution
By Charles R. Ashman, writer and professor of Constitutional Law. Nash Publishing, 1973.

The story of how justice is being poisoned by judicial pollution — by corrupt judges, their bribes, their broads, their fixes, their "loans" and all the rest.

Charles Ashman, a Constitutional scholar, lists documented cases that reveal names, dates, amounts and details of some of the most blatant corruption in American history and tells what can be done about it.

Melvin Belli says, "Charles Ashman is the most effective communicator and Constitutional scholar I know."

This book is not about insurers, but is aimed at the same judges that preside over the glut of insurance-triggered litigation clogging our court system.

Check the library.

CONGLOMERATES UNLIMITED
The Failure Of Regulation
By John F. Winslow, former counsel to the Antitrust Subcommittee of the House Committee on the Judiciary. Indiana University Press, 1973.

Winslow tells how one company may be acquired with the treasury of another and how insurance company assets may be raided.

THE LITIGIOUS SOCIETY
By Jethro K. Lieberman, Harvard Law School alumnus, Legal Affairs Editor of Business Week and author of several books. Basic Books, Inc., 1981.

Litigation is an excuse rather than a cause for larcenous premium rate increases. Insurers can "litigate a victim to death" then pick up the money and run. Exposed are a number of insurance swindles. Although critical of the excesses in litigation, Lieberman gives reasons why litigation is a necessary function.

128

There is a meticulously researched explanation of how the so-called medical malpractice crisis of the seventies was in fact malpractice by the insurance companies — an attempt to cover up huge losses of untaxed reserves gambled away on the stock market.

Fascinating and important reading for anyone interested in our court system.

★ MUST READING ★

SO YOU THINK YOU'RE COVERED

By Stanley Leinwoll, director of engineering for Radio Free Europe. Charles Scribner's Sons, 1977.

After personal experience with a residential fire the author became increasingly interested in the experiences of others, resulting in a book everyone should read for their own protection. He reports on the frustrations and hardships encountered by one family trying to return to a normal life in the weeks and months that followed their loss from a house fire.

Few property owners ever have their property repaired or replaced to their satisfaction. Even in cases where the companies honor their policies to the letter, homeowners must often wait months to collect on their claims.

Ambiguities in the policies and misleading terminology and phraseology make them virtually impossible to understand for all but an experienced few.

Advance knowledge of the dangers can be the best protection against the nightmarish problems that arise. Unfortunately, many people learn the hard way about settlement swindles *after* a loss.

Here is an easily understood book containing vital information for anyone relying on homeowners insurance for protection.

THE WORLD'S GREATEST RIP-OFFS

By top investigative journalists and edited by Colin Rose, educated at the London School of Economics. Sterling Publishing Company, 1978.

The extraordinary inside story of the biggest, most inventive confidence games shows that the dividing line between legitimate business and fraud is becoming very blurred.

A typical chapter tells of Wilson, a short fellow with soulful eyes, a weak chin, a strong sense of humor and a talent for directing frauds through offshore insurance companies, mortgage companies and banks.

This "short fellow with the weak chin" began by hustling auto insurance in a relatively honest fashion in Missouri, and capped his career with control of crooked insurance companies and related enterprises committing paper fraud from St. Louis, Missouri, to Mongolia, Moscow, Buenos Aires, Argentina, Panama, Australia, the Bahamas and even to the far reaches of East Africa.

Through control of offshore insurance companies and "desk drawer" banks, Wilson directed white collar crime on a worldwide scale. This book is the product of a powerful team of investigative journalists.

SUCCESSFUL HANDLING OF CASUALTY CLAIMS
By Pat Magarick, J.D., LL.M., V.P. Emeritus American International Underwriters Corporation; contributing editor, Insurance Adjuster Magazine and insurance claim consultant. Central Book Co. Inc., 850 De Kalb Ave., Brooklyn, N.Y. 11221, 1974.

This 823-page adjuster's training manual was written to help the claims man do a better job of investigating and reporting casualty claims. In the event of a "casualty," claims-jockeys arrange for the company to simply pay the claim "honestly and in full." Here are 823 pages of such simple honesty. The book was not intended to convince the human race it is being swindled.

Anyone faced with problems collecting a legitimate claim will find this fascinating reading.

THE CASE AGAINST NEW LIFE INSURANCE COMPANIES
By Halsey Josephson, C.L.U., noted authority on life insurance and author. Farnsworth Publishing Company, 1966.

Between the end of World War II and 1966, some 1,800 new insurance companies were formed. Fast-buck operations sprouted like mushrooms, with an average of about three new companies a week.

The 473 companies operating in the United States at the beginning of World War II understandably resented sharing the insurance pie with these upstarts. Halsey Josephson explains the reasons with shocking clarity.

"Well, $6.98 is very reasonable for insurance against attack, but I don't understand all this 150-diddle-deductible stuff in the tiny print."

An insurance weekly publication is quoted as editorializing in part, "Rumblings are being heard from many quarters...as this handful of ruthless operators muddy the waters."

New companies often are formed, staffed and controlled by money-hungry men underqualified for management or the work they are doing. Some companies have been launched by individuals with only the scantiest knowledge of how to run an insurance business. One chief executive officer came from the dry cleaning business, another was a grocer. Lawyers, clergymen, physicians and state governors have held executive positions. Testimony of state commissioners on the qualifications of fast-buck promoters will give the reader reason for concern.

A state insurance commissioner commented, "The boom we have witnessed is a powder keg, and the entire life insurance business is sitting on that keg."

This book contains valid criticism by a knowledgeable insider, despite the fact that he seems to soft-pedal the evils of the "mutual" monsters existing prior to World War II.

LIFE INSURANCE
America's Greatest Confidence Game
By J.D. Kidder, B.B.A., Certified Public Accountant. Printed in the U.S. by the George E. Minor Press and bound by Wiltsie Bookbindery, Seattle, Washington, 1938.

Here are authoritative facts about life insurance presented with the accuracy of a CPA. Readers who think they have heard it all are in for a surprise in these pages.

Kidder tells it like it was in the 1930s. Life insurers played the same centuries-old numbers games they do today, numbers games basically the same as the insurance offerings built into current "financial services." Then as now the companies maintained the attitude that they were above reproach.

An abundance of insurance propaganda has been directed to creating the misconception that cash value policies become more valuable each year. Nothing could be further from the truth. The cash value becomes higher simply because a portion of the overpayment for insurance has been applied to the "cash value" portion of the policy. *Death extinguishes cash values beyond recovery to the insured and his beneficiaries.*

The writer states:

We are now told of the benefits of the so-called Savings or Cash Value of a life insurance policy, and how much money we can have at sixty years of age. We are led to a big telescope which picturizes the citrus orchards of Florida, on one of which we are to retire and live happily ever after; through the mystic growth of the cash value of the life insurance policy we are urged to buy.

This is a very scarce, out-of-print book, copyrighted in 1938. We wish luck to anyone searching for it; those finding a copy will not be disappointed.

SHOPPING SMART
The Only Consumer Guide You'll Ever Need
By John Stossel, consumer editor for CBS TV's New York station, winner of seven Emmy Awards and graduate of Princeton University. G.P. Putnam's Sons, 1980.

The advice here on IRAs and Keogh Plans is, "Never buy one from an insurance company."

This book gives a verified report on a man who deposited $1,200 in an insurance company Keogh. When he needed money and asked to withdraw everything from his account he was told, "There is nothing in your account, all the money has gone to company fees and commissions."

Insurance policies are cleverly written in such complicated form it's nearly impossible to make price comparisons. Much of your policy money will never get back to you. It goes into overhead, fancy buildings, profits and to paying squads of salespeople who go out to gyp other people.

A well-researched, well-written and valuable book that will pay for itself in high multiples.

THE LIFE INSURANCE GAME
How The Industry Has Amassed Over $600 Billion At The Expense Of The American Public
By Ronald Kessler, investigative reporter for The Washington Post, *winner of fourteen journalism awards and formerly with the* Wall Street Journal. *Holt, Rinehart and Winston, 1985.*

Kessler does not say life insurance cheating is crooked beyond the wildest stretch of the imagination — he *documents* it!

This book began as a project for *The Washington Post.* It is an appalling report on the life insurance industry based on thorough research and exhaustive interviews with industry executives, agents and regulators.

For every dollar 2,100 life insurance companies take in from annual premiums and investment earnings, they pay out an average of just 14¢ in death benefits! This is the "Piece of the Rock" and the "Financial Umbrella" touted so highly by an industry that has amassed over $600 billion of other people's money!

Widows and orphans suffer severely because the average death benefit actually paid out by all types of life insurance policies is only $5,068.

A sixteen-page chapter explains in plain language how computers are used to bamboozle and rob as well as to benefit policyholders.

Another chapter tells a sordid story of insurance investigators known to gather reports on people's sex life. Some of their hearsay reports would make good reading in a pornographic novel.

There is no federal statute permitting consumers to review information gathered by these super-snoopers when investigating claims. They gather it as they wish, keep it as long as they want and sell it to whoever they want.

Chapter Nine gives mind-boggling information about industry profits and how they are invested. The man who presides over Prudential's investments rides through Newark's trash-strewn streets every day to decide how the

"I don't want to alarm you or rush you into a hasty decision, but one of my clients dropped dead and the coroner refrigerated his cadaver before he had a chance to sign an application. Think it over and give me your answer before I leave."

world's largest insurance company will allocate its wealth. Insurance decision makers can make or break a city, turn it into a thriving metropolis or a mortuary. They can run a stock through the ceiling or down to the cellar!

Kessler provides detailed information on slick sales methods used by seasoned agents; the control of regulators by the industry; how the poor are overcharged; how new type policies with "cash value" are just another way to spring the same old time-tested financial traps. Included is important advice on how to buy life insurance without getting stung.

This well researched book should be required reading for all policyholders and anyone intending to buy life insurance.

THE FOUNTAIN PEN CONSPIRACY
By Jonathan Kwitny, a Wall Street Journal reporter. Alfred Knopf, 1973.

Here is an exposé of a loosely-connected crew of inspired con men (most of them not in prison).

One chapter deals with insurance frauds and is recommended as a reference source in The Investigation Of White Collar Crime, a manual for law enforcement agencies from the U.S. Department of Justice.

It describes the swindler who can maneuver himself into control of a real insurance company, usually by paying for it with borrowed money or phony stock, and become master of that company's reserves. He can sell the company's assets for whatever he can get and replace them on the books with worthless securities.

Swindler-run companies have specialized in high risk coverage, all types of bonding and about anything else that leaves them in a position to take the money and run.

Con artists have eyed the "specialty reinsurance" type of companies that sometimes escape close attention from state regulators. Control of such companies is an invitation to withdraw cash as it comes in and replace it with fraudulent swindler-issued paper.

This informative book is still available in some public libraries.

THE CONSUMER'S GUIDE TO LIFE INSURANCE
By J. Tracy Oehlbeck. Pyramid Communications, Inc., 1975.

Here is a book crammed with facts exposing the catches and deception in life insurance literature and sales pitches. It will save you money and help you avoid financial traps.

Included is a warning of the expertise and razzle-dazzle sales techniques practiced to deceive and mislead uninformed buyers.

The epilogue blows the whistle on certain life insurance IRA swindles that have the industry licking its chops. It reports on the biggest moneymakers for the companies, which are indeed not the biggest moneymakers for you.

Must reading for life insurance buyers.

CONSUMER SWINDLERS ... AND HOW TO AVOID THEM
By John L. Springer, former editor for the Associated Press, author of several books on financial self-defense and articles in many major magazines. Henry Regnery Company, 1970.

Open this book, look for insurance swindles and you will be surprised to find that there is no mention of insurance anywhere in the contents. Look in the index and note there is no mention of insurance there either. How could insurance be left out of a book with such a title? You wonder if there has been an error in composing the index. Could insurance flacks have done the final editing? Whatever happened, someone failed to index insurance swindles, the granddaddy of them all.

Turn to page 175. Starting there you will find over three pages of condensed warnings about the trick clauses used by disreputable mail order insurance companies to rip-off the policyholder and at the same time avoid prosecution for mail fraud.

The subjects dealt with include phony veterans' life insurance solicited in brown envelopes similar to those used by the U.S. government; trick application forms to legalize nonpayment of claims; forewarning of the "No Medical Exam Required" gimmick; and hidden limitations restricting benefits and policies you may not collect on for the first two years even while you are paying premiums.

Essential reading for those who wish to guard against the gyp artist.

PART III

"HELL, WE'LL HIRE ANY WARM BODY"

And

"JUST CON THEM A LITTLE"

How Insurance Companies Victimize

Their Own Agents

As Seen By James Gollin, C.L.U.

In

PAY NOW, DIE LATER

"It's starting to rain, Al — warm him up fast,
before we short out!"

INTRODUCTION

"**H**ell, We'll Hire Any Warm Body" and "Just Con Them A Little" are reprinted by publisher's permission from *Pay Now, Die Later* by James Gollin, a Chartered Life Underwriter with a Master's degree in English from Yale University. These excerpts from Gollin's excellent book clearly show that policyholders are not the only suckers — a number of agents qualify for membership in that select group as well.

A high officer of an insurance trade organization and a senior vice-president of a major life insurance company approached Random House and asked to inspect the galleys of *Pay Now, Die Later* prior to its publication. Random House quite properly refused. The two executives indicated they would see to it that the book was kept out of the hands of as many life insurance agents as possible. When you read these chapters, you will understand why.

141

"We like them better when they're running scared."

—the Recruiter

3 . "Hell, We'll Hire Any Warm Body"

IN ORDER TO GET YOU—and 20,000,000 other people a year —to buy life insurance, every major insurance company is deeply committed to one technique only: the use of salesmen. Clearly, no industry committed to mass marketing on so vast a scale can possibly afford to depend on the efforts of a few supersalesmen. There simply aren't enough such men to go around. As far back as the turn of the century the market for life insurance had proved far too vast to be exploited·only by the natural-born sales artists. So even before 1900 this industry had spawned a complex organization known as the American Agency System, which could make use of the average man's abilities and capacities as a salesman. In theory—and there's nothing wrong with the theory —that's what any growing business has to do in order to keep on growing.

But life insurance isn't just any business.

In the first place, life insurance is too complicated for the average man to learn to sell. Second, and even more important, the average man cannot stand the physical and emotional strains of selling insurance. For most men, the frustra-

143

tion and rejection inherent in the job prove too severe to endure.

So an industry intent only on pushing ahead saw, and still sees, only one choice: to get the maximum possible mileage out of *unsuccessful* salesmen. The men who staff and operate the Agency System are taught, and later teach their successors, that it's necessary to enlist and exploit men whom they suspect and often know in advance will be total failures at selling life insurance. For the record, total failure means just that: the inability to earn a subsistence-level income which would pay the rent and put food on the table.

But there's more to this matter than the scandal of how the life insurance industry, through the Agency System, acquires, trains, and controls hundreds upon hundreds of thousands of salesmen. Because of this system, *both you and your salesman* have only the most tenuous relationship with the company that provides the life insurance. Because of this system, your own agent may be a failure—but more to the point, your life insurance is only a shadowy promise of what it could and should be. And yet, without the American Agency System, life insurance as we know it couldn't exist at all.

In a big company the Agency System is entrenched in the sales division. The Sales Department is headed by a senior officer whose subordinates are themselves vice-presidents. Each regional vice-president is in turn superior to district superintendents who purportedly supervise—and at least keep in touch with—the "line" executives in the field. Branch offices (or agencies) are spread out over the local, regional, or national areas in which the given company operates. Such agencies cluster in big cities, where one company alone might establish dozens of small-sized agencies, each in theory covering a territory of a few city blocks. Today agencies have sprouted in the suburbs also, where so many customers are now located. But the important companies serve even the least populous parts of the country through a sizable agency network. In all, there are tens of thousands of life insurance agencies. According to the census data available, only gasoline stations, restaurants, laundries, and other small retail establishments outnumber them.

Each agency is run by a manager. In the early days of the industry, the manager was a completely independent businessman, or general agent. His franchise simply provided that he would sell—usually on an exclusive basis—a given quota of life insurance for the given company. His methods of operation and his finances were his own business, and the company paid him a flat commission for every dollar of insurance premium he collected. But today most companies make salary arrangements with agency managers, keeping these field executives at least nominally within the domain of the company's sales organization.

The manager is the key man in the Agency System, for he's the one who controls the destinies of the men who do the selling. The manager hires these men, signing as the company's representative the legal contract that authorizes the salesmen themselves to act as agents for the company. The manager supposedly determines how all his salesmen should operate and trains new salesmen to work effectively. And it's the manager who has the authority to cancel a salesman's contract and thereby sever the man's business relationship with the company. The agency manager exercises more authority over his charges than most non-insurance executives, no matter how high up, ever wield.

The reciprocal duties and obligations of the manager and the company are prescribed by company rules and spelled out in contracts. But the rulebook can't cover everything. Moreover, in psychological as well as physical distance, the manager's local realm is far, far away from the company's

145

home office. Unless there's a crisis, the manager will have a free hand in running his operation. Both company and manager want it that way, and if things were different, the Agency System couldn't function. For the manager of a life insurance agency has only one basic job: to increase sales— this year, next year, and forever. The company doesn't really want to know what the manager does in order to keep on grinding out more and more new insurance—and the manager doesn't want the company to know. Therefore, between the agency manager and his superiors there's always the same unspoken (and certainly unwritten) agreement: keep on exceeding your assigned sales quotas, and you can write your own rules. Don't do anything blatantly fraudulent if you can help it; but above all, don't get caught.

One or more assistant managers is almost always at the manager's beck and call. Such assistants are managers in miniature, each one in charge of his own "unit," a group of up to ten salesmen. Assistant managers—who are all supposed to be longing for the day when they're given their own agencies—supervise the daily, and in some cases the hourly, routines of their men. In addition, as we'll soon discover, these junior executives have other highly significant duties.

One activity which all the agency's executives share is that of selling life insurance. Managers want to make themselves look good by adding their own sales to those of their salesmen. Also, selling is one way of earning extra money that meets with complete company approval. "Personal field work encourages the management team to keep its sales skills fresh," one management training manual says demurely. Because new salesmen "only respect managers who can do as well as teach," such personal selling supposedly makes it easier to train new men. So even if his management tasks do take up most of his time, a manager seldom hangs up his hat and quits selling altogether.

146

Finally, at the bottom of the ladder, we find—or we expect to find—the salesman himself. But unlike the agency manager and his assistants, the cashier, or even the girl who runs the switchboard, the insurance salesman is *not* an employee of the company he represents. Although you probably don't know it—and although your salesman himself may never have been told in so many words—the man who sells you your insurance is actually an "independent contractor," an entrepreneur running his own one-man business. Far more than even the lowliest typist or clerk, he is at the mercy of the manager and the company. He can be fired without the right of appeal, his business can be taken away, his career ended. His own rights are vague, and nowhere defined. In fact, his legal status is precisely that of a sharecropper or other contract laborer. And the treatment he gets from the company exactly reflects his status.

To substantiate this unsavory state of affairs and thus to understand the real nature of the salesman's lot, we must do our probing at the agency level—the level where a truly successful salesman is a rare bird indeed. Here's where the truth about the insurance business is really to be found, because the agency is designed to be a mill where through an endless process of enticement, trickery, and coercion, ordinary men are either converted into insurance salesmen or discarded. As we'll see, that process, starting from the beginning, is a mixture of comedy and anguish.

With the Agency System at its disposal, the company needs no special personnel department to select and recruit salesmen. That job is left entirely in the hands of the agency manager and his assistants, who have no choice but to be charming, persuasive, and ruthlessly dedicated exponents of insurance-selling as a career. The hunt for new salesmen will consume much of management's time and sweat. Holidays and weekends, when even the hardiest salesmen may tem-

147

porarily rest from the wars, the manager must be interviewing prospective salesmen, either experienced men new to his company or absolutely raw recruits. On the surface, the manager's methods should seem like the legitimate routines of any employer with jobs to offer. None of his techniques can appear to be unscrupulous. But nevertheless, recruiting methods and the philosophy behind them will come as a jolt to the uninitiated.

For example, the smart manager will cultivate everyone in town who might steer prospective salesmen his way. Ministers, educators, and social leaders all make good "nominators" of potential recruits. Such "centers of influence" are cultivated mostly with blarney but sometimes with gifts or cash. For each situation the manager will work out a special approach.

He'll also build up his own private grapevine to keep abreast of any discontent among his competitors' salesmen. If he does any personal selling, he'll use his best salesmanship to extract the names of likely sales candidates from his customers—and at the same time proselytize the customers to become salesmen themselves. He'll use anything from back-scratching to subtle blackmail among his friends and *their* friends. A hungry manager on the prowl for new recruits makes his own salesmen seem genteel by comparison. One manager even teaches a night-school insurance course, "strictly because I can do eighty per cent of my recruiting right in class."

In training his assistants, the manager will sometimes instruct them to take charge of the agency's head-hunting for a given period. Assistant managers may be matched against one another to see who can bring in the most new men. Often each assistant is given a quota to fill on behalf of his own unit.

With the enthusiastic approval of the company, many

managers offer a bounty of $50 or $100 to an established salesman for each seriously interested candidate he turns up.

In a small town, where the local agency manager is likely to be prominent, more personal recruiting methods are generally the most effective. A clever and persuasive manager can get away with audacities which would make a run-of-the-mill recruiter a laughingstock. But he must also be careful about his recruiting so he won't have to face the accusing stares of local men who have failed after being talked into the life insurance business.

The real head-hunting and body-snatching in life insurance recruitment, and the most unprincipled hustling, all go on in the large cities, where the process of filling up the agency's roster of "rookie" salesmen is almost mechanized. Where there is a steady stream of men to exploit, the manager can reduce his recruiting effort to another version of the numbers game that insurance men are always playing. For example, the urban agency can rely almost entirely on advertising as a source of prospective salesmen.

SALES CAREER—Salary $400–$700 + com. Outstanding opty for highly motivated man who has owned his own business or served in mgmnt capacity either sales or administration.
SALES, PRUDENTIAL INSURANCE CO.—Immediate salary and training. $6,000–$9,000.
EXECUTIVE SALES POSITION—$750 per mo salary + comm 2 yr contract. We will train you (insurance). Coll or sales exp pfd. For a man of $10,000 yr calibre.

Any man who has ever looked for a job has seen advertisements like these in the Help Wanted columns. Such ads are run daily or weekly by the agencies of many different companies, and each insertion will bring in its share of responses. Once in a while some outfit will try what it thinks is a more sophisticated ad, like the following, which appeared in the business section of at least one Sunday paper in New York.

149

WANTED: Extremely intelligent, highly articulate, independent minded executive age 35–45. The man we're looking for must be successful, aggressive, willing to take direction but still and all very much his own kind of guy. We're specialists in developing such men into professionals in the fields of employee compensation, estate analysis, and business planning. If you think you qualify, call or write . . .

This gem wasn't meant to be spotted by an outsider as a life insurance recruiting ad.

In fact, about half the ads run by insurance agencies suppress the information that the job is an insurance-selling proposition. The idea is to tempt into the agency those men who normally wouldn't even dream of seeking such a job. Other managers explain that the job involves selling life insurance because "we only want repliers who know what it's all about." To a neutral observer, the results seem about the same either way. Besides, that *suppressio veri* is only a little white lie alongside the real lies the advertisements tell. And the mendacity of the ads is as nothing compared to the deceitfulness practiced in turn by the agency's recruiter once he gets a live candidate inside the door.

The recruiter leaves simple instructions in case anyone calls or writes in response to an ad: have the man come in. "Hell, we'll hire any warm body," one recruiter explained. "We don't want résumés, we don't want to exchange letters. We want to get our hands on the man, whoever he is." His philosophy could hardly be more explicit: he's in the business of *hiring*, not selecting, salesmen.

The first steps of the recruiting process are relaxed and seemingly informal. When the candidate arrives, he's shown into a comfortable office and given the usual employment-and-personal-history blank to fill out. Then he takes a test. Even the most violent anti-test crusader would have to laugh at the test given to prospective life insurance salesmen.

True, this sales-aptitude test was designed by a recognized supplier for the Life Insurance Agency Management Association, and since its inception the test has been updated several times. But the test is meant to take little longer than forty-five minutes, and for anyone with even the mildest interest in becoming a life insurance salesman, it's almost impossible to give the wrong answers. (In at least one agency a friendly secretary is on hand to supply hints to candidates the manager particularly wants to hire.) Within moments after he finishes the test, someone tells the candidate that he did extraordinarily, amazingly well. In contrast to the seriousness with which these tests are given by most non-insurance employers, this situation is farcical.

Many home-office and trade-association experts claim to believe in these tests, and to them, the farce is naturally disturbing. Faced with the continuing need to add more salesmen, however, most agency managers put no faith whatever in tests or testing. Besides, even an effective test would be licked from the start. If necessary, the manager will falsify test results before putting them on the record of the man he may hire. "All we really want to know is whether the candidate can read," one assistant manager, not particularly cynical, commented.

But the real reason for these tests, as far as the manager is concerned, has nothing to do with screening out undesirables. Like everything else about recruiting, the test is only another stage in the process of persuasion. It's used to *sell the candidate* on the care and attention this company supposedly gives to picking salesmen.

Once the test is out of the way, the candidate is moved on to the next phase, a lengthy interview with the recruiter. Any real screening or selection is done here. As in a life insurance sales interview, the recruiter, who certainly must himself be a good salesman, will make sure his prospect is a normal

151

individual, and not, for example, an obvious unemployable, a seasonal job-seeker, or an antisocial type. Beyond that, it's helpful if the candidate is (1) fairly presentable, (2) intelligent enough to learn something about insurance sales, and (3) in rather urgent need of a job. Aside from this last point, it seems as if almost any American can qualify for selling life insurance somewhere, just as almost any American can usually qualify for buying it.

Here, by the way, we can pinpoint the first lie told by the recruiting ad, which so often stipulates that a man must have previous sales, management, administrative, or other executive-level business experience. No such qualification is necessary; it's enough to have held down almost any job (or for that matter to have been jobless). The presumably more sophisticated agencies in the big cities give some preference to the white-collar candidate, and respectability is obviously an advantage. Mentioning all those "executive" posts in the ad is just another way to make insurance work seem attractive.

During this first interview the recruiter will attempt to learn something about the candidate's personality and general background. The interviewer may also begin to spell out the appealing reasons why the candidate should choose insurance sales as a career. But the real recruiting pitch can't begin until the agency staff learns a little more about the candidate, so this interview ends with a promise to "let the man know." The candidate leaves with a pocketful of literature about the joys of an insurance man's job; and there's a hiatus of several days in the recruiting process.

In this interim the candidate's statements about himself will be checked and his previous employment record confirmed ("investigated" is too strong a word; it's just the usual once-over-lightly credit report). Then the entire dossier will be scanned by management. The thoroughness with which

152

this part of the process is conducted depends on company requirements, on the urgency of the manager's need for the candidate, and on how recently the agency has been stung by a fraudulent applicant.

As soon as the candidate's background is checked, the wheels begin to grind again. The candidate—if he hasn't changed his mind or found another job—is summoned back, this time for a series of shorter meetings with various members of the staff. In a small or new agency this procedure might involve one or at most two interviews. But in a better-established "shop" the candidate will make the rounds of a number of assistants before winding up in the manager's office.

In those agencies which have developed recruiting into a real art, the recruiter will have the candidate "drop in on" a successful salesman who "happens to be in the office" that day. The salesman will chat with the candidate and perhaps "tell him how things really are" in the life insurance business. (The salesman is there by prearrangement, and his "frank discussion" with the candidate sometimes comes out of a book.) If the candidate joins up, the salesman may earn a cash bonus or at least be in line for a case of whiskey or some theater tickets.

These interviews are designed to make the candidate feel at home, to impress him with the general air of prosperity and good spirit, and to disarm him of any skepticism he might feel about the job he's being wooed so hard to accept. Moreover, this "all-around-the-agency" pattern is meant to pique the candidate's curiosity and set up an atmosphere of expectancy. There must be something special about an industry which takes so many pains with prospective employees, the agency wants the candidate to think. Here I've been filling out forms, taking a test, being interviewed, and meeting executives in the best job-hunting tradition—except

153

that *here* they've treated me as if I were important. The candidate probably won't notice that the warmth of this welcome is slightly impersonal and the agency's enthusiasm somewhat forced.

And he wouldn't be human if he weren't still curious about those promises in the recruiting ad: the generous starting salary, the training program, and the chance to progress into management.

So when he finds himself sitting in the manager's office, the candidate is usually still eager to find out what will happen next.

What does happen depends on what the manager has learned about him from written reports and his assistants' comments. The interview also depends on the manager's own favorite recruiting tactics, his personal acquaintance with the candidate (or the candidate's friends), and a whole host of other intangibles. Some managers don't even like to conduct this interview at the office. Like many other modern pitchmen, they prefer to do this part of their job over a luncheon table or at dinner.

The candidate will find himself listening to a velvet-smooth sales presentation conducted by an expert whose sincerity and conviction will be impressive. The virtues of life insurance, the rich rewards of a selling career, and the promise of an exciting future will all be spread before him; and the manager's favorite phrases to describe such delights will ring sweetly in his ears.

The shrewd manager won't attempt to hide the fact that the life insurance business has its drawbacks. But, the manager will always add, the problems of selling life insurance only serve to bring out a man's best qualities: perseverance, courage, industriousness, intelligence.

"Of the men I've recently met under these circumstances," one manager loves to say to his spellbound candidates, "it

154

seems to me that you"—he pauses for emphasis—"may well have the most natural ability. And I really believe that together we can give you the opportunity to grow, to enhance your life, and in case you're not a charitable institution"— he smiles—"make you, frankly, richer than you ever dreamed you'd be. So how about it? Will you give us that chance?"

This particular manager is unusually fluent and imaginative. For the manager who doesn't trust his own persuasiveness, there are many texts to memorize. Selling the life insurance career has its own canned spiels, just as selling insurance does.

If the candidate finds the manager's rhetoric stirring, he may even sign a salesman's contract right on the spot. Some of the manager's promises may be a little vague, and some of the candidate's questions may go unanswered. But—so the candidate thinks—there's no reason why such details can't be straightened out later. The important thing for us to keep in mind is this: the candidate is probably out of a job and anxious for new employment; or the candidate may have been recommended to the agency by a friend or some person he has reason to trust. For one reason or another, the prospective life insurance salesman—unlike his more skeptical relative, the insurance customer—will very often want to believe the things he's being told.

So the new candidate agrees to come into the life insurance business. The recruiting stage is over, and the hiring stage begins. This consists of two simultaneous procedures: (1) the more or less mechanical activity of taking on a new recruit and (2) a certain amount of further psychological "preparation." To deal with the second matter first, the new agent must now be convinced that he's made a wise choice. Equally important, his wife must also be convinced, because life insurance is one business in which the salesman's wife can really make or break him. The long hours, endless de-

155

mands, and possibility of economic strain all have to be made as palatable as possible.

The astute manager will hasten to make friends with the new employee's wife. The chances are that he'll invite the couple to dinner at an expensive restaurant and exert every ounce of his charm to convince her that the future will bring wonders for her and her family. At the same time, the manager will be sizing up the relationship between husband and wife, filing away in the back of his mind opinions about the lady's intelligence, taste, and willingness to co-operate. Many wives find such attention both obvious and distasteful, but that won't faze the manager.

One reason the Agency System regards this wifemanship with dead seriousness is that the wife, according to management folklore, sets the economic pace for the marriage. "We want a man who's frankly running a little bit scared," one manager states. "If the wife has expensive tastes and wants to live well, she'll push the man better than we can." And most managers also know that regardless of whether a man is succeeding or failing, a discontented wife can mean real trouble.

Becoming an insurance man also calls for other, more usual employment routines, such as passing a medical exam and moving into an office. And now, of course, is the time for the new recruit to be confronted by the question of money. What did that ad say about a salary?

"That's our special system of field compensation," the manager will smoothly explain. "Under this system a new man draws whatever salary he needs. So for the first three years—and if you want, even longer—you'll be taking home a regular pay check, with raises and bonuses based on your production. Now, I see you've been making five hundred dollars a month. Suppose we start you at six hundred . . ."

After this little speech the manager will slide across the

desk three copies of a contract. The recruit, still bemused by the casual way he's just been given a raise, will undoubtedly put his name on that contract as eagerly as a mouse puts his nose in the trap. Needless to add, he won't read a word of it; and even if he did, he wouldn't understand it.

He won't understand the all-important fact that the *company doesn't consider him an employee at all.* Small wonder. What better evidence of employment is there than a contract? The last thing our new man suspects is that *his* contract enlists him, legally speaking, in the ranks of the *self*-employed. And he certainly won't realize that as far as money is concerned, the manager's explanation tells something other than the truth, that his contract really spells out a system of getting paid that's as different from a salary as chalk is from cheese. The new recruit isn't getting a salary at all. Like every insurance salesman since the beginning, he's earning straight commissions.

Traditionally the insurance salesman (or "agent," as we should now begin to call him) has been awarded commissions on the assumption that he must be paid not only for selling life insurance but also for keeping the insurance in effect and up to date once it's sold. As soon as the customer pays his first year's premium charge, the agent is allowed a hefty first-year commission. Even in conservatively regulated New York State, this commission can run as high as 55 per cent of the annual premium. When the insurance owner pays his subsequent yearly premiums, the agent receives a more modest "renewal commission." Under the standard commission schedule, renewal commissions— which usually come to 5 per cent of the premium each time —are payable for a period of up to nine years. Thus, "fifty-five and nine fives" is the salesman's stock phrase for describing how he gets paid. It's no coincidence that this formula

157

yields a total commission exactly equal to one year's premium.

With this commission schedule in mind, we can puzzle out the problem that the new recruit won't face until it's too late: How can a man supposedly paid only on a commission basis possibly receive a salary? The answer is he can't.

If we remember that there's a nation-wide shortage of salesmen and an even more desperate shortage of men willing to sell insurance, the whole situation makes better sense. For this means that in getting salesmen, the insurance industry must compete against businesses that not only pay salaries but offer generous fringe benefits as well. As we know, the life insurance industry doesn't believe in salaries for its salesmen (let alone paid vacations, sick leave, or anything else). The industry doesn't believe in *employing* salesmen in the first place. And yet, the companies do have to recruit somehow.

So within about the last ten years the Agency System has devised an ingenious way of "reconciling" the two opposites: the *commission* arrangement that the industry likes and the *salary* it despises but is forced to offer as bait.

This new method, which is in fact a supplement to the standard commission contract, goes by the name of the "validation agreement."

Superficially this agreement resembles the old-fashioned "drawing account" used in other commission-sales businesses. Under the usual drawing account, a salesman can request his employer to pay him a regular weekly or monthly sum out of the commissions he's earned. That way the salesman can make sure his money lasts between sales. Some employers will even let a man "get behind on his draw" and go into debt to the company if they expect the salesman to recover his financial health shortly. By and large, a drawing

158

account is a helpful adjunct to commission earnings—at least for an experienced and money-wise salesman.

But the life insurance industry thrives on inexperienced and unsophisticated men.

So its validation agreement is advertised as a "salary," or even more dishonestly as a "salary plus commission," not as a version of the drawing account. Of all the lies recruiting ads tell, this one is the most flagrant. Many companies further the deception by calling their validation agreements "salary plans," and the recruiter will beguile the new candidate with the term "salary" until the contract is signed. Both the legal and the psychological point of no return has usually been passed before the new candidate discovers that his so-called salary is in fact no such thing and that his status as an employee is entirely illusory.

Two key points of the validation agreement make the new man's situation painfully clear:

(1) The agent must sell, within a given period, enough life insurance (and thus earn enough *commissions*) to justify, or "validate," the money advanced to him regularly as "salary." If the salesman doesn't make the grade, the "salary" stops. Then, in order to get paid at all, the man must switch to a straight-commission contract. If he gets far enough behind even before the given period is up, the manager has the authority to withhold the "salary" anyway, at least until the man makes up the difference.

(2) Under a validation agreement the agent relinquishes all legal rights to the commissions he earns. If he quits (to change companies, for example) or he's fired while he's ahead, he forfeits all of what he hasn't yet drawn. If he leaves while behind, he can't take a nickel with him, even if his renewal commissions will clearly exceed his actual indebtedness.

With a stick like this in his hand, the agency manager has every reason to believe that hiring and then controlling new

159

salesmen will be easy. It must be admitted that along with the stick the manager can also manipulate the carrot. By adding bonuses or special "extras" to the commissions actually earned, the company can make some investment in the salesman; and most companies, however grudgingly, do so. However, such bonuses aren't paid directly to the man who earns them ("You think we're crazy?" one manager queried). Instead, they're thrown in with all that other money the salesman can't take with him if he leaves.

But most important, the business end of the validation agreement is a formidable bludgeon for the manager. After hooking his new man with a generous starting "salary," the manager can then keep the salesman under constant pressure until he's used up. Threatening to cut off the salesman's income is only the most obvious form of pressure. A manager who really knows the fine print in that validation agreement can easily develop such special kinds of leverage as arbitrarily *increasing* an agent's "salary" (a step that uses up credits already earned) and then working the man mercilessly to make him stay even. Another common variation of the basic theme is to "survive" a poor salesman if he happens to have good contacts. By a little fast shuffling of credits between salesmen's accounts, the manager can accomplish this at no cost to the agency. Once the manager has uncovered and exploited the victim's prospective customers, the man can be dumped unceremoniously.

True, the insurance company must protect itself against being sued by an agent or former agent whose manager is a bit light-fingered. But most companies don't really care what the manager does with the salesmen's validation accounts. They do penalize the manager if too many agents quit while they're far behind. But the truly resourceful manager *never* tells the indebted salesman that legally he has no obligation to pay back such arrears. Instead, when the agent

160

leaves, the manager makes him sign a personal note for whatever is "owed." This the manager collects himself, and —since the company doesn't expect repayment—he quietly puts the money in his pocket.

To the untried salesman, justifying a "salary" beyond his reach can obviously become a nightmare. To have that contractual sword of Damocles hanging over his head does occasionally make an effective salesman out of a new man. But much more often, the fear of this sudden-death loss of income forces the beginner to sell insurance in ways that make even hardened veterans shudder. One man, for instance, found that the only way he could sell enough life insurance to validate his salary was to offer a rebate (i.e., a kickback) to his customers. Since rebating is a criminal offense in the state where he operated, every time this poor devil sold a policy he ran the risk of being turned in. He also ran the risk of being blackmailed by his customers. Sure enough, somebody did call his illegalities to the attention of the State Insurance Department. As a result, the man not only lost his agent's license and was fined enough money to bankrupt him, but was also sentenced to ninety days in the workhouse. (Mercifully the sentence was suspended.) He never did find out who informed against him. But his comrades in the agency knew that the informer was none other than the agency manager—who was disgruntled that the salesman wasn't kicking back enough to *him*.

Such utter rascality isn't necessarily the rule. But in almost every one of the thousands of life insurance agencies, salesmen are driven to commit fraud and near-fraud in order to keep on validating their so-called salaries. The agent who is under such pressure finds it temptingly simple to falsify his figures. He knows that his customers will never find out. For instance, he can quote a lower price than the policy actually costs, apologizing for his "error" later on. If the

161

salesman is glib enough, you may willingly pay the few dollars' difference—forgetting that over the years the difference will cost hundreds of extra dollars. Or the agent may claim that "dividends will lower the premium substantially," knowing that you'll forget to check the actual dividends against his original projections. He may sell you a policy that pays *him* a higher commission—and costs *you* much more than you need to spend. And you'll never know; for just as he is at the mercy of his manager, so are you at his mercy.

Some insurance-company executives and even a few decent managers privately admit that despite its value as a recruiting gimmick, the validation agreement is nothing but a legalized fraud. "We'd be much better off telling the new guy what really lies ahead," one executive remarked. "Then at least he wouldn't hate life insurance when he failed." Yet this executive's company has one of the most deceitfully effective validation agreements in the industry. But you must realize that a big company sees its salesman in the same statistical terms in which it sees everything else. By fair means or foul, so many men are recruited, so many hired, so much insurance is sold, and so many men are terminated. Only the sales statistics really matter. The success or failure of the individual salesman means nothing whatever.

At this point the new salesman is feeling his way into a novel, unfamiliar, and grimly unique business environment: that of the life insurance agency. As our picture of what goes on at the agency level begins to take shape, one thing will be obvious. Given the manager's motives and requirements, plus the recruit's own needs and burdens, it's not surprising that a life insurance agency is a peculiar place. It's filled with people who shouldn't be there, and thus the scene of perpetual personal crisis.

"No matter what you do, most of these men will fail."

—*the Vice-President*

4 . *"Just Con Them a Little"*

MOST PEOPLE NEVER HAVE OCCASION to set foot inside a life insurance agency or to visit an agent at *his* office. Even if we did make such visits, our impression would more likely be one of bleak efficiency than of anything darkly satanic. Nevertheless, the assembly-line process of converting *people* into *insurance agents*—which this chapter explores in depth —is an unfunny parody of exactly what we might expect to find in an old-fashioned mill: creaky machinery, relentless pressure on the hired hands, and an appalling amount of failure.

Because the products of the Agency System's thousands of such mills are the men who sell us our life insurance, there's a special and highly personal reason for us to venture behind the scenes. If the insurance man is the victim of his own system, then every time we buy or even contemplate buying insurance, we become victims of the same system.

Our brand-new salesman will notice at once that half the desks in his agency are empty, many of its cubicles vacant. Everybody's out selling, his supervisor will quickly explain. "You can't make any money sitting at a desk" is Lesson No. 1 about being a life insurance man. The logic of that lesson

163

will seem apparent, and later in the day the salesmen will begin to drift in and fill up some of that empty space. For quite a while the new man won't know just what most of these men really do with their time.

During his first few days on the job, the new man won't have much chance to think about anything he sees, because his own time will be as thoroughly programmed as that of a child in summer camp. The recruit's first efforts are divided between reading about insurance and being taught how to sell it.

So his morning hours are typically spent in classes, where, along with the other new men, he'll learn as much about insurance as the class supervisor, the agency, and the company want him to know. Teaching methods range from informal lectures and chalk-talks to elaborate audio-visual presentations. In recent years the entire life insurance industry has espoused the idea that "employee communications consultants" do a better job of sales training than the industry's own staff experts. Such outside firms lean heavily on films, recordings, and similar aids to enliven their "curriculum"; so life insurance men increasingly acquire their primary education from a movie projector. "It's certainly not the agent at one end of the bench and Mark Hopkins at the other," one serious-minded insurance educator remarked drily, when asked about the quality of this machine-teaching.

In essence, the new man is taught a somewhat more elaborate version of the factual material set forth in the first chapter of this book. But the emphasis is on the purely practical: how to compare one policy with another, how different forms of insurance can be tailored to fit a customer's real or imagined needs. At this point the Mandarin jargon of life insurance becomes the salesman's second language. He learns to think and speak in terms of "living values," "protection," and other euphemisms of sales promotion. Simultaneously the new agent picks up the technical vocabulary of his trade and begins to bore his wife with talk about "interest layback," "contingent beneficiaries," "dividend options," and similar quasi-professional gobbledegook. By the time he's finished his basic training, the new man won't know any other way to talk about his product.

Aside from his labors in the classroom, the recruit is given homework. On his very first day at the office he's handed a couple of thick, neatly indexed loose-leaf binders full of information about the company, its products, and the art of selling life insurance. He also receives what will become his Bible, the company's pocket-sized book of rates and technical information. For the two to three weeks that his basic training continues, the recruit's evenings at home will supposedly be spent in perusing this material, in completing written quizzes on insurance, and in learning how to use the ratebook.

The pages of that little book are covered with figures, and each set of figures tells a different story. A given company will provide sixty or seventy separate forms of life insurance for every age between zero and seventy. (Above seventy, rates must be obtained from the home office—along with special permission to sell the insurance.) The salesman who "knows his way around the ratebook" is thought to have an enormous advantage over a competitor who has trouble handling his own figures. Using that book, a brand-new man can work out the details of any given policy in about ten minutes. After a few months he'll be able to do it in seconds.

Unfortunately, the man who has mastered this purely mechanical chore is usually assumed to possess as much knowledge of the product as is necessary. The beginning of real insight into life insurance is a sense of the way simple

165

laws underlie some very complex arithmetic, a feel for the
mathematical logic that relates life, death, and money. But
most new insurance men aren't encouraged to think in such
terms at all.

The new man's training is more concerned with other
matters. For example, the company's philosophy is sure to
be spelled out in the first section of the salesman's training
manual. The entire vast company organization, so the recruit is told, came into being in order to answer a great need
and to serve the public. The company's management is likewise dedicated to this task. The basic requirements for success in the life insurance business are scrupulous honesty,
hard work, and above all a selfless dedication to the service
of the insurance-buying public. Testimonials, inspirational
texts, and even Biblical quotations underscore the virtues of
such success and conclude on an upbeat the new man's initial dose of assigned reading.

It's easy to laugh at this approach, especially in the light
of what we already know about the life insurance business.
But beginning insurance men naïvely do want to do good,
and this fact provides management with powerful motivating and incentive-building opportunities. If the new salesman can be convinced, at least for a while, to take up his
calling with missionary fervor, then training him presents
fewer problems. The more idealistic a man is at the start,
the easier it is for him to swallow the Agency System's basic,
if insidious, rationale: *insurance is so beneficial that almost
any means of selling it is entirely justifiable in the long run.*

As early as his seventh or eighth day in the business the
recruit is handed a special notebook. "Open the book to the
page headed Names of Relatives," the supervisor orders.
"Now, there are fifty blank lines on that page. Some of you
have small families, but everybody has at least fifteen or

166

twenty relatives—cousins, brothers-in-law, uncles. Jot down their names."

The supervisor moves on rapidly to cover close friends, acquaintances, fraternity or lodge brothers, college classmates, business contacts, church groups—until the whole range of possible acquaintanceship has been covered. When the routine is completed, the new man almost always asks just what these names are for.

"We want you to sell every one of these names life insurance!" the supervisor replies enthusiastically. "Those names belong to people who need insurance and want insurance. Look at it this way: How would you feel if a friend of yours died suddenly and left his family without enough money to get along on, *and you hadn't spoken to your friend about life insurance?* What would you say to your friend's widow if she asked you, 'Joe, why didn't you make John buy insurance?' "

Nothing could demonstrate more clearly than such indoctrination what management really wants from the new salesman. The new man must himself be sold the idea that life insurance is a universal need. Having bought this concept, he can then be pressured into exploiting his own personal relationships for insurance purposes—as long as those relationships last.

To have the new man start with the inventory of people he knows best (and presumably has the best chance of selling to) is certainly the easiest way for management to make him productive. And the more friends and relations the new salesman can sell, the better—because it's a foregone conclusion that most of the recruits will ultimately fail. As far as getting the most out of them is concerned, the agency manager is trained to think in terms of weeks and months, not of years. So the salesman must be made to start with his own list of clay pigeons.

After filling up his notebook, the recruit is instructed to transfer all those names onto file cards and thereby systematize his stock of potential customers. He'll now have to remember his prospects' addresses, telephone numbers, and useful personal history. Which of his friends recently suffered a death in the family and is therefore in the right frame of mind to consider buying insurance? Who might be generous enough to throw a little business his way? As soon as this information-gathering has begun to yield a supply of names, and while the new man's self-confidence is at a peak, the recruit is ready for his moment of truth.

He must now attempt to sell his first life insurance policy.

For many men this very first sale is no real test, because some relative or friend makes things easy for the fledgling. "I hear you're in the life insurance business, Joe," goes the friend's kind-hearted speech. "Well, I do need some insurance and I'd like to help you out, so come on over and write me up a policy." This unbusinesslike event can happen often enough to postpone a recruit's real tribulations until after he's made a total commitment, emotional and financial, to the business.

As a rule, the new man's supervisor accompanies the recruit on such order-taking interviews and actually makes the sale while the recruit watches and listens to learn how it's done. Under the circumstances, selling life insurance seems like a cinch. But the time soon comes when the new insurance man runs out of obliging friends and relatives and has to begin dealing with less obliging ones. Against such a day, he has been trained to use other methods.

"Paul? This is Joe . . . Fine, thanks, and you? . . . Paul, as you may have heard, I'm now in the life insurance business, and while I have no reason to believe you're interested in adding to your program at this time, I do have access to certain ideas and information which may be of value . . ."

The recruit is sitting at his desk in the bull pen with a stack of his index cards in front of him. Propped up so he can read from it is a three-page printed folder entitled *Successful Telephone Techniques*. After a couple of hours' practice with his supervisor the new man is trying to use what he's learned, with his acquaintances as guinea pigs. Chances are that this is his first real selling effort; by now he's been in the life insurance business about ten days. The folder with his script printed on it is made of stiff cardboard. As the new agent—palms sweaty from nervousness—makes his calls and delivers his spiel, his voice sounds stiffer than that cardboard. But (if he follows the printed sales talk) not even the rawest recruit will discuss *insurance* over the telephone. "You can't sign up your prospect on the phone," reads the exhortation on the folder, "so forget about life insurance and sell the interview."

". . . Paul, it would only take about twenty minutes of your time to learn how these ideas would apply in your particular case. Could you give me the courtesy of that amount of time Tuesday afternoon at four, or would Wednesday morning be better?"

To render artificial phrases fluently requires the same diligence as learning to be a Shakespearean actor. Those agencies that take selling by telephone seriously conduct actual seminars in technique. "Be Natural!" one booklet on the subject exhorts. "You can put a smile in your voice if you put a smile on your face. So relax, think of something pleasant, and let that broad smile appear."

The sight of a room full of salesmen, each one talking into the telephone with a wide smile on his face, can be disquieting, to say the least. And when the party at the other end of the line begins to make things difficult, it can be hard to keep that smile pinned securely in place.

"Well, I certainly can understand your being busy at this time of year, Paul. But my ideas won't take up more than a few minutes..." or,

"Well, frankly, if you told me you *were* interested in life insurance, I'd faint dead away." (Chuckle) "But my ideas and information could be of value to you in case you ever contemplate a future purchase..." or,

"Paul, just about everybody has a brother-in-law in the business, but maybe my ideas and information can show you how to make your present insurance more valuable..."

The above, of course, are the printed answers to three of the most common objections the solicitor hears: (1) too busy, (2) not interested, and (3) a relative in the business. In every case, the salesman is supposed to answer the objections by asking once again for a definite appointment. "Statistics prove," that folder states, "that most interviews aren't granted until the request is made four times."

"Well, look, Paul. I plan to be in the neighborhood on Tuesday anyway. Suppose I stop by and spend a couple of minutes with you, just to shake your hand." If this doesn't work, nothing will, and the recruit is instructed not to try any further. (The experienced man rarely prolongs his efforts this far.)

By the time this first telephone session is over, the recruit is usually exhausted both physically and emotionally. But he'll have learned something about the realities of insurance that nobody will have told him before: it's tough to make a sale.

For many a new man, alarm replaces self-confidence after he calls the first half-dozen friends to tell them the glad tidings of his new career—and finds them a good deal less friendly than he'd expected. This is the recruit's first ex-posure to "insurance agent's syndrome," a roller-coaster al-ternation between moods of optimism ("My cousin was a push-over") and fits of depression ("I can't get an appoint-ment to save my life"). A single half hour on the telephone is usually more than the beginner can stand. After such a session some recruits flatly refuse to do any more telephon-ing at all that day. But most new men take comfort in the cheery words of the supervisor. "You had nine turndowns in a row? Well, you're only one more no away from a yes!" The supervisor knows that the recruit must develop a rea-sonably good telephone manner—as well as weather this first experience of rejection.

So the shrewd unit manager sits in the bull pen with his recruits while they make their calls. He jokes about the answers they're getting, rejoices at a success, analyzes why a man is having trouble ("Slow down, Joe, and *smile,* smile until your face cracks"). He'll make the whole nerve-racking ordeal as much like a game as possible, running contests be-tween recruits, buying coffee, letting the men take frequent short breaks. As with anything else, there's an art to running a successful bucket shop—and that, of course, is exactly what this is. Gradually the jolt of rejection will trouble the recruit less, and this plus a little success in getting appoint-ments will restore some of his self-assurance. After a week or two the recruit will doggedly work on the telephone for sev-eral hours a day. But no insurance man ever *likes* telephon-ing, and some men develop reactions which are positively neurotic. For instance, after a particularly grueling afternoon —seventy-six calls, zero appointments—one rookie tore his telephone loose from its connections and flung it at the su-pervisor. "Then," this former agent remarked with gusto, "I went out and got stoned."

171

As he spends more time on the telephone the recruit learns that his supply of friends, relatives, and acquaintances won't last forever; the logistics of telephone solicitation see to that. A persistent man can make fifteen to twenty telephone contacts per hour. About one third of the people he's trying to reach will for one reason or another be unavailable; so he'll actually talk to ten to fourteen people. If he makes even one appointment, he's lucky. Four or five hours on the telephone will use up sixty to eighty names; and therefore, even the friendliest recruit soon begins to run out of people to call. So even while he's still sifting through his circle of acquaintances, management has begun to drill him in other ways of finding prospective customers, such as begging for prospects, as well as sales, from the people he already knows.

"George, let me ask you a question. Suppose there were a way you could guarantee income at retirement to a friend of yours, or guarantee your friend's son a college education —without its costing you a cent. You'd do it, wouldn't you? .... Well, all you have to do is introduce me to three of your friends . . ."

First the salesman sells an interview. Then he tries mightily to sell insurance. And finally, whether or not he succeeds at his primary task, the salesman is supposed to sell his customer the idea of referring him to others. This is the standard Agency System method of training the salesman to keep himself in circulation.

Ideally such a "referred lead" system should work wonders for the salesman because the system enables him to call only on people who know in advance who he is and what he's selling. The salesman who conscientiously asks to be referred to new prospects should never run out of people to see. But in practice, this "endless chain" technique rarely works for the new man.

People may be willing to buy their own life insurance from the new salesman, but most people are understandably reluctant to turn a life insurance agent loose on their friends, and an inexperienced agent at that. It's not as if insurance men were hard to come by—so the usual reasoning goes— and besides, sending an insurance man to a friend is a little bit like sending him a present of soap: an unfriendly reminder.

Nevertheless, in training agents, the manager and his associates still put great stress on endless-chain prospecting and getting referred leads. The reason is obvious: such methods are easy to teach and cost next to nothing. Moreover, these strategies require no special marketing knowledge on the supervisor's part and demand no insight into the individual agent's qualities and capabilities.

Thus, once he uses up his supply of personal contacts and finds that referrals are hard to come by, the agent realizes that as far as seeking new customers is concerned, he's very much on his own. His discovery of this fact may coincide with the discovery that he's on his own in most other ways, too. Management has furnished him with minimal facilities for learning about life insurance. His agency has provided rudimentary training in how to sell. The recruit has a desk, a mailing address, a telephone—but nothing more. In return, management has gained the new man's willing cooperation in knocking down a few easy birds. Those three or four sales to friends and relatives have already more than repaid the expenses of the company's "investment."

And thus, in three weeks to a month the honeymoon is over.

At this point decent management men may sympathize with the not-quite-so-new salesman. The new man's immediate supervisor may now explain, or try to explain, the rationale underlying recruitment, hiring, and training. But the moment has come when the agent must be told that he's got to look after himself. Besides, by this time there's a newer crop of recruits to process, and there isn't much a busy supervisor can do for this month-old veteran.

No wonder one company vice-president sums up the new agent's predicament by stating flatly that "between the first and the sixth month a new man's survival is largely a matter of luck." It takes something special to withstand the rigors of selling life insurance. The unconcern of the management about the given agent's sales success adds another load to his burden. And the agent who does survive learns that at this stage, success consists of a series of tiny triumphs and slender prizes.

Thus, it's a victory to steal or charm an interoffice telephone directory from a receptionist because a company phonebook is a good source of names. When he begins to pull other names from the society or business columns of the daily papers, the new man tests himself in competition with dozens of other salesmen. Wedding, engagement, birth (and death) announcements and reports of job promotions or changes are the common gleaning ground of a community's new insurance men. If you get married, switch jobs, buy a house, or have a baby and you've been unwary enough to make the fact public, you'll be a target for every hungry agent in town.

For the new salesman, every telephone call is an exercise in self-discipline. Every interview is a cause for celebration. And every policy sold is a do-or-die effort, often for only the most modest cash return. At the best of times, to deliver the sales message in the necessary relaxed style is a challenge. To do so while full of worry about that validation agreement is almost impossible. And yet, customers don't want to talk about life insurance with a desperate salesman.

Those who survive during this initial period attribute their success in large part to one thing: outside economic resources. "I didn't inherit any trust fund," one now established agent commented, "but my wife was working, thank God, or we'd have starved."

But in the life insurance business, survival tactics depend on more than luck, extra income, or the ability to conceal insecurity behind the salesman's mask of perennial assurance. In *The Organization Man*, William Whyte recollects an old-fashioned sales manager who said to a group of budding salesmen, "Always remember that the man on the other side of the counter is your *enemy!*" At this point in his career the life insurance man forgets about the niceties and learns to channel his frustration, fear, and anger into effective salesmanship. After I'm established, he tell himself, I can afford to be a public benefactor.

Gradually he masters the art of making contacts. Where half an hour of telephoning once left him limp, the salesman can now make phone calls all day long. However, in learning how to use the telephone efficiently, he again finds himself up against a problem in logistics. "I spend so much time on the telephone," said one salesman plaintively, "that I don't have time to see the people I'm calling." If it sometimes takes four hours of telephoning to produce a single interview, the salesman has to work a forty-hour week simply in order to go to work. As a way out, the agent will very likely turn to an even more mechanical way of securing prospects: direct mail. This in turn entails drudgery of a very different kind because it's up to the agent to supply himself with mailing lists and do (or pay to have done) the coolie labor of addressing and mailing out his literature.

175

Nevertheless, most salesmen eventually do send out letters, purportedly from the company's executive offices, which not only offer insurance information but promise a free gift—anything from a memo pad to a road atlas—if the recipient returns a reply card. Except that too many who reply are interested only in the memo pad and not in life insurance, such mailing pieces do provide a steady, automatic way of prospecting for customers. The really hard-boiled agents dispense with such frills as free gifts and send out the cheapest, crudest form of direct mail they can buy. "I'm not in the memo pad business," one agent observed tartly.

Even the most desperate life insurance salesman avoids door-to-door canvassing like the plague. "What do you think I am," he'll demand if his supervisor suggests such last-ditch methods, "an encyclopedia salesman?" However, there are times when a man will do anything. "We used to go into those tenements, stand in the hallways, and yell 'Seguros'—Spanish for *insurance*. If anybody stuck his head out the door and hollered 'Si!' we'd climb the stairs and make our pitch. Until the company made us quit, we were making six or seven sales a day that way." Such methods may seem out of date, to put it mildly. But this agent was merely describing what he did to sell life insurance in New York's *barrio*, or Puerto Rican ghetto, in 1961—and salesmen go through similar routines every day all over the country. You can imagine what it meant to this agent—a college graduate with years of business experience behind him—to have to peddle his wares in the slums.

The rare individual who can thus drive himself past humiliation stands a good chance of growing into an effective operator—as in fact the "*Seguros*" agent has done. Out of necessity such a salesman will learn how to cajole some customers and bully others. But he'll also learn how to be con-

176

vincing. Gradually the numbers of sales he makes will increase; and after one year, or two, or three, the agent will find himself meeting the quota and perhaps even justifying his starting "salary." After five years (or longer), he'll still be working a sixty-hour week and he'll still be out most nights and week ends. The salesman will have adjusted his personal habits accordingly, as part of the job—in short, he will have survived. But while the threat of outright failure haunts him less, success continues to recede before him like a mirage.

According to an authoritative agent training manual, "The average successful salesman of life insurance . . . earns $4,000 a year in first-year commissions." Taking into account renewal commissions and extra allowances, this means that such a salesman will eventually reach an average level of income of $7,500 to $8,000 a year, with a maximum (after about twenty years) of $10,000. It's no coincidence that once a salesman reaches this $4,000-a-year commission mark, many companies admit him to "production clubs," paying his way to conventions, and the like. Agents making this kind of money after ten, fifteen, or twenty years of hard labor are the stalwarts on whom the industry and the public depend. But to many of us, an insurance man's "average success" will seem like little more than bare subsistence.

The grim vocational truth about the insurance agent's calling is that survival is no guarantee of success. On the contrary, the Agency System's version of a career more nearly resembles a treadmill. If a man does keep his balance climbing on, he then gets a chance to go on running in the same place forever.

The crowning irony is that the very methods the agent must use in order to survive are almost certain to block him from achieving any real success, as most of us understand

177

the term. For the insurance man who does drag himself up to that average-successful level can almost never acquire the knowledge and background necessary to sell insurance on a really substantial scale. His earnings will be based on the sale of small or medium-sized policies to small or medium-sized customers. And in order to maintain those earnings, the average-successful agent must work unceasingly at the thing he knows, pushing life insurance. So he has little time or energy left with which to dig into the complexities of a business world outside his daily routine, and his *savoir-faire* will never be equal to dealing with really important customers.

Persuading the sharp-eyed executives, lawyers, and accountants who make insurance decisions not only for themselves but also for their well-heeled clients demands something more than persistence and will power. To work with such sophisticated buyers requires detailed, specialized knowledge. Any insurance man who aspires to the most lucrative market for his product must know tax and commercial law, business analysis, and economics. He must, of course, be supremely versed in the intricacies of insurance itself. Finally, this salesman must be able to socialize and conduct easy business relationships with the people he wants to make his customers. This means behaving superbly in the soft-spoken role of the consultant, and exuding professional authority and objectivity. How many life insurance agents can meet such standards?

In recent years an organization called the Million Dollar Round Table has obligingly made public the results of a continuing survey of its membership. As the name implies, the MDRT is composed of men who regularly sell $1,000,000 worth of life insurance or more a year. In fact, according to an MDRT brochure, "The Million Dollar Round Table is one of the most exclusive 'clubs' in the world . . . comprising only about *one percent* of all life insurance agents!" The organization's 1965 survey drew answers from 2,000 of its 4,500 members, which should place its statistical accuracy beyond question. And up to a point the statistics of success do speak for themselves.

Among these leading salesmen, the annual income averages about $29,000 and ranges from under $10,000 to over $150,000. About two thirds of the MDRT's members earn between $11,000 and $40,000 a year; another 23 per cent earn between $40,000 and $75,000; and 10 per cent earn over $75,000. Even allowing for the fact that in some cases a good deal of this income is derived from non-insurance sources, the million-dollar salesmen make good money at their trade. And from additional information in the survey, it's apparent that these salesmen operate in ways that have little to do with standard Agency System training. For instance, the average MDRT member makes fewer than twenty phone calls a *week* for interviews. Yet the MDRT agent sees 20 per cent *more* prospects than the average man, and he sells fifty to seventy-five policies a year, a very high average.

Such statistics do appear impressive; and they prove that despite the Agency System, some men at least can make a real career out of selling life insurance. "Why, these men are outstanding individuals," was the reaction of one guest at a special MDRT convention. "They're not like life insurance salesmen at all!"

But that remark merely drives home one absolutely crucial point. The true significance of the foregoing statistics, and indeed of the Million Dollar Round Table itself, is that in the life insurance industry only a disgracefully small handful of agents ever reach the top. (Moreover, we should note,

179

this *crème de la crème* aren't as rich as all that. To be sure, the $29,000 average yearly income is eminently respectable, but not so startlingly high in an era when in other businesses hundreds of thousands of men, not just the top handful, do equally well.)

To the consumer, yet another point is equally crucial. The best men whom this industry's survival-of-the-fittest methods produce are a small group of prosperous salesmen plus perhaps another small cluster of competent men who never quite enter that charmed million-dollar circle. Beyond that, we have the thousands upon thousands of average-successful agents.

And so, in life insurance most people, if they're served in any meaningful fashion at all, are served by men who don't even come close to being successful in their own right.

What this really means to us as individuals is a subject reserved for full discussion later on. But here we can at least sense the nature of the problem. If the product in question were some tangible item—an appliance, a car, or even a house—most of us wouldn't care or ever need to care about the economic well-being of the man who sells it to us. If the dishwasher breaks, the car refuses to run, or the roof springs a leak, we have easy recourse to people who can straighten things out. But who fixes stupidly, incompetently, or dishonestly arranged life insurance?

According to the industry and the Agency System, we must look to the insurance man as the expert. To ourselves and our families, the agent is presented as an ex officio financial consultant who is especially reliable in case of an emergency. "The New York Life agent in your community is a good man to know," we read in one magazine ad. A competitor suggests, "Don't answer until you've talked with your Prudential agent, a 'real pro.'" But what kind of help or

180

advice can we expect from someone who was hired in the first place because "he was running a little bit scared"? How trustworthy about our most intimate financial problems can any man be when his own financial future depends on making us buy something *right now?*

The statistics of success only remind us that as insurance buyers, millions of us must settle for the exact opposite of success. Indeed, every time the life insurance industry points with self-satisfaction to its "exclusive club," the MDRT, most insurance buyers have every right to be angry. Because a successful agent is so hard to find, we can conclude that the American Agency System has a great deal to answer for.

To understand how much trouble this system really causes, we should proceed to examine as best we can certain other much less accurate statistics. For there are figures that agencies do their best to hide from their parent companies, figures which these companies in turn conceal from their own top managements and from their competitors, figures that the industry shrouds in deep secrecy.

These, of course, are the statistics of failure.

Up to now, we have been filling in the portrait of an industry that sustains itself, and indeed thrives, on every single degree of unsuccess. Yet even though we may fully expect the worst, the ugly facts of failure in the life insurance business will still come as a shock. Of the approximately 110,000 men and women recruited, hired, and trained *each year* to sell life insurance, some 90,000—nearly 90 per cent—leave the business *within ninety days.* And by the end of each full year, year after year, another 5,000 to 10,000 have failed.

True, these aren't the figures that circulate within the industry. According to official sources, the "turnover ratio" among salesmen is much lower. Some of these sources estimate the ninety-day turnover rate as 65 per cent, and *The*

New York Times (in a 1965 article on tests for new recruits) cited surveys that give this rate 50 per cent. But with salesman turnover as with much else, this industry's officialdom demonstrates a remarkable capacity to minimize problems. Company sales executives are well aware that their agency managers falsify personnel records (for instance, by keeping agents' contracts on the books long after the men themselves have vanished from the scene). Companies themselves are anxious to whitewash their hiring and firing records. "We certainly don't feel that this is anything the public needs to know about," one high official said.

But whatever the exact percentages are, it's absurd to quibble about the statistics of disaster. For failure still overtakes the huge majority of those who enter the life insurance business. Even if the men who failed were few in number or of low calibre, such high *percentages* would be cause for bitter concern. But an appalling fact about this turnover is that so many of the men who fail are decent, enthusiastic recruits, not drifters or white-collar bums.

These fearsome statistics can't reflect the individual experience of failure, misery, and defeat a man tastes—often weeks or months before management actually intervenes—when he realizes that his efforts aren't going to make him successful. Theorizing about failure is a favorite hobby at every level of the industry, but no serious research has been done to learn why agents fail. The reason isn't far to seek. Nobody really cares to know.

"Most men fail because they don't do the automatic things. They don't send out mail, they don't telephone, they don't sell to their friends, so naturally they don't stay in the business." This is the agency manager speaking. To him, the recruit fails because he doesn't do the mechanics of the job, and superficially, of course, he may be correct. But most managers are also well aware that some sort of emotional disturbance (a disturbance of which the salesman himself may be completely unaware) underlies this reluctance to perform. But the manager's *own* training manuals preach the usual nonsense about "motivating" men with pep talks and certainly don't tell him anything worth knowing about why a man's energy and spirit may suddenly flag.

It's a pretty sure bet that the manager has himself been a fairly successful salesman and has the successful businessman's contempt for bad performance. Furthermore, somewhere along the line most managers have devoted hours of time, counsel, and personal help to agents who have thwarted their efforts by failing anyway. A few such experiences can harden even a compassionate manager's heart and beckon him to guard his psyche by hiring new recruits instead of sweating out the salvation of the old.

So for the most part, agency managers are content to talk about failure in the stale, old-fashioned, black-and-white terms that other businesses have long since discarded. "George has everything it takes to succeed. Trouble is, he's lazy. Joe over there could make it, too. But he's yellow, scared the customer will turn him down." Even those managers who presumably know better are still quick to identify laziness and cowardice as the *primary* causes of failure.

If we took these managers seriously, we would have to believe that every year 90,000 to 100,000 men drop out of life insurance business because they lack industry or are afraid. You can't find many executives willing to pass such contemptuous—and false—judgment on men they had courted assiduously a few months before.

Now let's turn to the companies themselves, where computers digest the sad facts of failure and spew them out as unemotional statistics. Here, high-level executives view

183

the turnover figures with professional unease and—so they tell one another—work hard on ideas to improve matters. Significantly, however, their grand schemes are almost always aimed at recruiting *more* agents, so that the turnover problem won't ever affect sales. Any uneasiness these executives do feel is only that of businessmen whose methods aren't working as well as they should (though some of these executives act like men who definitely don't like being reminded of what their methods really produce).

For example, consider the reaction of one extremely able management official. As dispassionate as he usually is, this gentleman waxed at first argumentative and then irate on the subjects of recruiting and turnover.

"Look here," he said finally. "As an occupation, selling is held in low esteem in our society. And among all the sales categories—heavy equipment, food, and so on—life insurance selling is well down the list. This means there are only a limited number of men we can attract to our sales jobs.

"Whether we use fair means or foul, out of all the men we do attract a small percentage is going to beat our system and make a pot of money. As for the rest, it doesn't matter a damn *what* you do, pay them a real salary, double their commissions, or serve them breakfast in bed. They're going to fail."

In one form or another, these sentiments are echoed by dozens of executives throughout the industry. "We're sucking hind teat in the job market, and that's all there is to it," one official explained. His counterpart in another home office rephrased things a bit more elegantly: "It takes a special combination of skills to sell life insurance. Only a few men have these skills, so we're always going to have the problem of failure."

Yet despite their firm—and curiously, almost pleasurable

184

—conviction that endemic failure has to be the salesman's lot, some of these executives are also defensive about the problem. "Why pick on us?" is one of their favorite questions. The same executive who was quoted at length above was very eager to point out that other direct-sales industries (whose products range from encyclopedias to home improvements) have equally bad or even worse turnover records. In fact, according to this official, the life insurance industry is in pretty good shape by comparison.

But that other businesses practice equally unscrupulous tricks on the men they hire or display equally regrettable turnover ratios doesn't excuse the life insurance industry. Telling lies, offering phony security, and causing human wastage is vilely wrong. The life insurance business has no right to defend its dubious methods on the grounds that other enterprises do worse. On the contrary, this industry claims that its dedicated agents stand sleepless guard over the financial security of millions of Americans. That's enough of a reason why life insurance men should be immeasurably better-trained, more capable, and more secure than the men who offer, say, vacuum cleaners, cosmetics, or aluminum siding to the public.

In the end, most insurance executives shrug aside such charges, and defensive or not, justify the Agency System on the grounds of past successes and present expediency. As bad as they are, we're advised, the industry's sales methods have worked for seventy-five years. Today the public endorses the Agency System by the most direct means of all: buying billions of dollars' worth of insurance a month from its representatives. It's a pity—so goes the industry's refrain —that any large-scale distribution system must involve such waste of time, money, and human resources. But that's part of the price you must and will pay to have life insurance.

Year by year, millions of us buy life insurance from agents who won't even be around long enough to send their customers the insurance man's obligatory Christmas card. It's a stock joke in any life insurance agency that the average customer buys insurance seven times—from seven different agents. And that insurance men themselves think such gallows humor is funny speaks volumes about the quality of the service we can expect from the men who sell us our insurance.

Even the uncommon man who prides himself on the skill and thoughtfulness of his own agent pays a ransom each year to the Agency System. As that good agent is the first to admit, *somebody* has to pick up the tab for so much failure. Somebody has to pay for the dropout salesman and the high cost of distribution. That somebody, of course, is the public. We should expect to pay for the privilege of dealing with a specialist about a matter as personal and important as our life insurance. But must our contributions support instead an agent we can't trust and a system most of us would gladly change if we could?

Apparently so. At present the Agency System is still for most Americans the only game in town. But (as we'll be discovering in the next chapters) for many of us the range of choice is beginning to widen. A partial solution to the evils of the Agency System is already being written in various government offices, in the headquarters of huge pension and welfare funds, in corporation insurance departments, in banking and investment centers, and ironically, in many divisions of the life insurance industry. Even though this system continues to hold its sway over life insurance, its time may be running out.

EMPLOYMENT AGENCY

"Colossal Benefit Insurance Company? You advertised for an executive trainee with experience in marketing protection to small business concerns? Well..."

PART IV

"DECEPTIVE MERCHANDISING"

One Chapter From A Report On The Premium-

Payer-Be-Damned Attitude Of Profiteering

Health Insurance Companies

As Seen By John E. Gregg, Ex-FBI Agent, Lawyer

And Repentant Former Instructor/Trainer Of

Health Insurance Salesmen

In

THE HEALTH INSURANCE RACKET AND HOW TO BEAT IT

INTRODUCTION

This chapter focuses on phony "group" insurance plans that rob **labor union members** and bamboozle union executives. Attention is directed at mail order swindles, **"Christian" insurance** in the Bible Belt and the built-in policy features that frustrate collection of claims.

Although the comparison tables included date from the 1970s, the inequities exist today in even more sophisticated form.

2

Deceptive Merchandising

THE merchandising of health insurance has become a very sophisticated operation. Door-to-door salespeople continue to make their rounds, but mail order promotion is becoming more and more profitable. While mail order is a boon to the insurance company, it can be anathema to the buyer. Except for face-to-face misrepresentation, mail order is the main source of deceptive insurance selling, even fraud.

While much of the alleged insurance fraud today involves smaller companies, it is nevertheless wrong to equate volume with quality. The giants* are better at protecting their image. They are sufficiently opulent to shun the more obvious swindles that offend the public.

---

*The fifteen largest companies, listed in Dunne's Insurance Reports, are as follows: Aetna, Connecticut General, Connecticut Mutual, Equitable of New York, John Hancock Mutual, Massachusetts Mutual, Metropolitan, Mutual Benefit, Mutual of New York, New England Mutual, New York Life, Northwestern Mutual, Penn Mutual, Prudential, and Travelers.

All Commercials, giants included, use the same discriminatory underwriting practices, which were formulated more than three decades ago. All likewise fail to control costs, with the Blues and giants setting the pace on premium increases. Policies by giants, like those of the midgets, offer only partial benefits. All private health insurance organizations ignore the poor and those classified as medically unfit.

The large and reputable companies that pioneered the field and led the industry to where it is today cannot be exempted from the responsibility of providing quality health coverage at decent prices. They have the resources to guide us out of the health insurance abyss in which we are trapped.

Opposing federal regulation, the giants insist that the industry must be self-policing. They therefore have a strong responsibility to correct abusive merchandising by establishing voluntary standards through a code of ethics for all companies. If the companies are to remain unregulated, however, they had better move quickly; public disgust with insurance companies is bringing mounting pressure on Washington for a federal takeover.[1]

Insurance historian Albert W. Atwood[2] says that even some of the giants have been caught with dirty hands. In 1877 a New York State legislative committee found Equitable, New York Life, and Mutual of New York guilty of wholesale political bribery. (Although the hearing transcript disappeared, William J. Manning published it—only to have the companies buy the whole printing.) In 1905 the New York Legislature discovered that officials of several giants were perpetuating themselves in office through forged proxies on nonexistent policyholders.

Mississippi Insurance Commissioner Walter Dell Davis summed up insurance morality in one statement, made at a misrepresentation hearing. An insurance company lawyer had said, "I believe that my clients are reasonably honest."

Davis floored him with, "I agree that they are just as honest as times and circumstances permit."[3]

Mail Order Selling

Mail order health insurance companies are flourishing at an unprecedented rate as people grasp for something to help them meet mounting health care costs. Hundreds of companies are in the act. One family received these mail solicitations in one week:[4] (1) a Safe Drivers Hospital Plan for $1, first month; (2) a cash Refund Token to apply on a savings account $100 weekly hospital plan; (3) a Big Check Information Certificate to return for free information on a $100 a week "money-back hospital plan GR 77C"; (4) the American Association of Retired Persons $100 a week Hospital Plan B; (5) a Medo-O-Matic plan exclusively offered to senior citizens; (6) the Updated Plan of the Engineering Society of Detroit; (7) Globe Life's Auto Driver's Accident and Hospital policy; and (8) the American Ordinance Association's Double Security Program.

National Liberty Corporation, parent company of National Home, and Union Fidelity—both Pennsylvania members of NALC—appear to be setting the pace on volume of mail order advertising. Both company heads (Arthur DeMoss, National Liberty, and Harry Dozer, Union Fidelity) freely discuss their mail order philosophy and say virtually the same thing: mail order insurance success derives from fear motivation and the public's desire to get something for nothing.[5] National Home's eight-page multicolored supplement advertising its $500 a month hospital policy for twenty-five cents is scare-saturated:

> One out of two families will have someone in the hospital this year. It could be you—or some beloved member of your family—today—next week—next month. Sad to say, very few families have anywhere near enough coverage to meet today's soaring hospital costs.

Both DeMoss and Dozer claim credit for originating their advertising, which takes one or more full newspaper pages of crowded print to promote a simple hospital indemnity policy. They discovered that people respond better to a lengthy advertisement. According to Dozer, "The more they read, the more sold they become, and they get the impression they are getting a lot for their money."

Each man claims to have the largest mail order budget and more mail order advertising experts than the other. They both say that great care is taken by their "legals" to comply with all laws. Seeing a bonanza in the average person's fear of financial disaster from oppressive health care costs, they are moving quickly to convert fear into fortunes.

Listening to these great merchandising geniuses discuss each other leaves the distinct impression that a personal vendetta is underway. This vendetta has resulted in the most ostentatious advertising binge in insurance history.

Group Sales

Sales specialists realize that Americans are joiners. Most workers and retirees belong to one or more organizations —professional, civic, religious, fraternal, trade, labor, retired persons, farm, civil rights, patriotic, veterans, and so forth. Most such groups have been—or are about to be—reached by insurance merchants.

While the heterogeneous membership of such organizations usually makes "true group" health plans impractical, they are natural markets for individual and "franchise group" policies. True group insurance involves a master contract between underwriting insurance companies and employers or other duly constituted legal entities, such as chartered labor unions. Individual employees or members are not actual parties to the contract but technically are beneficiaries under the master policy. They are issued certificates that outline their benefits and identify family members or dependents who are covered. An outstanding advantage of true group protection is reduced costs; employers or group administrators actually collect and remit the premiums to the insurance companies, frequently in the form of a monthly check.*

Many civic, trade, fraternal, and other voluntary membership organizations do not have the facilities to collect premiums from their members. Nonetheless, insurance companies see these groups as natural markets for mass selling. To capitalize on this market potential, the industry invented the term "franchise group." In reality, this is not group insurance at all but merely a method of exploiting voluntary membership organizations to mass-sell individual policies that carry few, if any, of the advantages of true group insurance.

Members of various organizations are solicited by mailings and membership publications that seek leads for salespeople. Agents contact those who respond. Mailing expenses plus sales commissions make this method so costly that the companies are now trying to go direct, asking members to complete their own applications. This is dangerous business since most people are not trained to know the significance of health history on an insurance application. If they omit "pertinent health," the companies plead fraud and deceit at claims time.[6] Unfortunately, even many writing agents are ill-equipped to handle the delicate business of health underwriting in the field. New agents—especially those who sell for only one company —are indeed fortunate if they receive one full day of training in this crucial area. Their initial training, which seldom lasts as long as a week, is directed almost exclusively at prospecting, memorizing canned sales talks, and

---

* See Chapter 11 for the advantages of true group insurance.

"closing," with very little emphasis on product knowledge. Nevertheless, each new salesperson is given a "health underwriting guidebook," which contains instructions on how to handle most health problems encountered in the field.

Persons with no training or instruction who complete their own applications have no way of knowing what health history to include or how to record it. Most buyers are better off dealing face to face with even poorly trained agents than attempting to fill out their own applications.

Organization members and others buying by mail are led to believe that savings accrued from mail order selling are passed to them. A standard advertisement states:

> How can we offer all this protection for so little? UNION FIDELITY ENROLLS A LARGE NUMBER OF PEOPLE AT ONE TIME. . . . This highly efficient "mass enrollment" keeps underwriting, processing, and policy issue expenses to a minimum—cutting our costs to the bone.[7]

However, savings accumulated through mail order sales go to the companies, not the buyers, as is shown by Table 2. The table shows comparable policies, one sold by agents and the other by mail.

Even apart from questionable advertising, these $100-per-week hospital policies hardly seem worth considering. The American Hospital Association puts 1969 average hospital costs at $69.93 per patient day, and 8.3 days is the average stay.[8] Most of these policies have an "elimination period," some seven days, some shorter, some longer. For the average hospitalization a $100 weekly policy with a seven-day elimination would yield $14.28 (fractions of days don't count) against a $580.42 hospital bill—with nothing for doctors, surgeons, drugs, and special services.

Third-Party Endorsement

Before companies can approach the members of a group, organization officials must be persuaded to cooperate.

Table 2. Comparison of Policies
Sold by Agents and by Mail Order

Guarantee Trust Life $100 per week hospital policy sold by agents		Union Fidelity Company $100 per week hospital policy sold by mail order	
Ages	*Monthly* *Premium*	*Ages* *(men & women)*	*Monthly* *Premium*
Men, 19-35	$4.00	19-39	$3.80
Women, 19-35	$4.50		
Men, 36-50	$4.50	40-54	$4.80
Women, 36-50	$4.95	55-64	$5.80
Men, 51-65	$4.60	65-74	$6.80
Women, 51-65	$5.20	75 and over	$9.10

This is the coveted "third-party endorsement." Attaining this cooperation is called "set-up work," requiring tact, diplomacy, and persuasive selling by the best "front" agents in the business.* Organization officials must tell their members that the insurance company designed a special program tailored to solve the insurance problems of the membership. The scheme's success hinges on the members' belief that they are getting a special deal at cheap prices. This impression is usually untrue.

Three of the many organizational types that are often exploited by insurance schemes are fraternal order, labor, and religious groups.

Fraternal order. The following letter was recently mailed to all members of a large fraternal order at the request of insurance salespeople:

Dear Sister and Brother:
    For some time now we have received requests from our members for a cash hospital plan that would pay extra cash

---

*This author was a general agent doing set-up work and training others to do this work.

and supplement the coverage our members now have through group insurance and even medicare. We knew that there are many practical and economic advantages for such a program, but we wanted to be sure that we had *a plan fitted to our membership needs* [emphasis added] and a company large and respectable enough to fill those needs.

It is therefore a pleasure to announce the sponsorship and endorsement by the Grand Lodge of the New Hampshire Independent order of Odd Fellows, of a plan of hospitalization insurance *that has been designed for us* [emphasis added] by Health Underwriters Agency, Inc., a widely known group insurance underwriter. This plan is underwritten by Union Fidelity Life Insurance Company, Philadelphia, Pennsylvania, which is well known throughout the entire nation.

Enrollments are now being accepted. All members and families, and widows of members of the Independent Order of Odd Fellows and Rebekahs may enroll regardless of the amount of insurance they currently have or will have under Medicare. No age limit.

The plan's success depends upon the whole-hearted support of our membership. It is a privileged opportunity for us to participate, and we urge you to take advantage of it.

The letter introduces a brochure describing a "remarkable Cash Plan that pays you $100 a week when you go to the hospital...."

As the New Hampshire I.O.O.F. solicited its members, the Union Labor Division, Life Assurance Company of Pennsylvania (Philadelphia), mailed the identical advertisement to Tennessee labor unions. The cover letter, slightly changed, said:

It is therefore a pleasure to announce a plan of hospitalization insurance *that has been designed to fit the special needs of organized labor and their families* [emphasis added].

The plan is underwritten by Life Assurance Company of Pennsylvania, which is well known throughout the entire nation.[9]

In all respects, including prices, the "special plan" for unions was the "special plan" for Odd Fellows.

During this period Union Fidelity was mass-mailing a "plan designed especially for residents of Mississippi." It was the identical plan designed especially for New Hampshire Odd Fellows and Tennessee unions.

Contemporaneously, Union Fidelity ran full-page advertisements throughout the country announcing a special plan "for people of all ages." It was, of course, the same plan tailored for New Hampshire Odd Fellows, Tennessee Union Members, and residents of Mississippi.

After scoring in New Hampshire, Union Fidelity moved rapidly to secure endorsements from I.O.O.F. Grand Lodges in Arizona, California, Colorado, Connecticut, Idaho, Kansas, Kentucky, Michigan, Minnesota, Missouri, Montana, North Dakota, Nebraska, Ohio, Oregon, Pennsylvania, South Dakota, Wisconsin, and Vermont.

Labor. Organized labor, with over 25 million members who habitually work for regular pay, is probably the country's most coveted insurance market. Members clock in daily if they are able to get out of bed. Unions have current mailing rosters, and, as a result of collective bargaining, they are health insurance-conscious. This is a near-perfect combination for protection merchants.

In its newsletter to unions American Income boasts single-minded devotion to "specially designed health coverage for union members who are in good standing." Its 1969 annual report stated, "Accident and Health premiums increased approximately one million dollars, to $8,315,000, a 13 percent increase for the year." The company started growing in 1963 after moving seriously into the union field, where it also sells special "union labor" life insurance. Its 1963 income was slightly over $5 million; it increased to $15 million in 1969, mostly from union members.[10]

Guarantee Trust Life, formed in 1936, showed mediocre results until setting up its union labor division in 1964. Its 1969 annual report announced "new and unique marketing programs" and showed the following growth after adding its "union labor line":[11]

	Surplus	Assets	Premium Written
1960	$ 512,567	$ 4,408,741	$ 9,091,129
1964	1,131,889	7,224,438	16,639,814
1967	1,659,124	12,245,860	18,411,433
1968	2,002,067	15,066,389	19,398,130
1969	2,736,129	18,215,461	20,491,624

Other companies that have cracked the union market include Amalgamated Labor Life, Bankers Life of Indiana, Combined Insurance, Mutual of Omaha, First Continental Life, National Casualty, Old Equity, and numerous others.

The standard approach is to form a Union Labor Division simply by printing *Union Labor Division* on letterheads, policies, and advertising material. Salespeople usually avoid mentioning the company name.

Union labor insurance merchandising has become standardized through the exchange of information by the companies and their agencies. The usual self-introduction by an agent is, "I am with the Union Labor Division, which has been established nationwide to bring special benefits to members in good standing. Our costs are lower due to mass enrollments of unions, but our coverage is much better than anything on the open market." Little, if any, of this spiel is true.

Benefits in "special union labor policies" usually are downgraded, while premiums are 25 to 100 percent *higher* than are those for policies sold to the public. Guarantee Trust sells its Form 22170 R disability policy "exclusively to members of labor unions in good standing." American Income's GNF 65 is almost identical. Guarantee Trust's disability Form 2020 is sold to nonunion applicants. The basic benefit in all three policies is $200 per month for disability. Table 3 suggests that "union policies" discriminate against union members.

The approach can, at best, be termed misleading. At the start of a campaign, for example, members get announcement letters like the following, which was mailed for Guarantee Trust on the stationery of the International Brotherhood of Boilermakers, Kansas City, Kansas.

Dear Member:

This is to announce a SPECIAL UNION MEMBERS IN-SURANCE PLAN for you. We have arranged for every member to be offered this Union Labor Insurance at a very low cost.

The program has been approved by the State Insurance Department and is available only to union members in good standing with their Local.

Here are just a few of the Special Benefits:

1. You are protected 24 hours a day—*at work, at home,* or *at play.*
2. Will pay you up to $200 a month from the first day of medical treatment for sickness. House or hospital confinement not required.
3. Will pay you up to $200 a month from the *first day* for accidental injury producing disability.
4. The benefits double while you are in the hospital due to sickness or accident. For example, if you are covered by the $200 plan, you will receive $400 a month while in the hospital.
5. Pays your beneficiary up to $2,000 in event of accidental death.
6. *Arbitration privileges*—any claim disputes can be referred to a Board of Arbitration for settlement.
7. *Waiver of Premium While on Strike*—premiums falling due during an authorized strike are waivered.
8. Full benefits paid regardless of other insurance or Workmens Compensation.

Table 3. Union *vs.* Nonunion Policies

	PREMIUM RATES				BENEFIT LIMITS		
	Mo.	Qtr.	Semiannual	Annual	Duration of Sickness Benefit	Duration of Accident Benefit	Accidental Death Benefit
American Income and Guarantee Trust, $200 monthly benefit Special Union Labor Disability policies	19.70	58.55	114.00	220.96 (American Income) 219.20 (Guarantee)	2 years	5 years	2,000.00
Joining fee: $10							
Guarantee Trust, $200 monthly Benefit Disability policy sold to nonunion employed persons	15.00	44.10	84.60	150.00	Lifetime	Lifetime	10,000.00
Joining fee: $20							

There are many other benefits, including *Guaranteed Renewal Warranty*. But the benefits are too numerous to list in this letter. You will want to know all about them and you can—simply by putting your name and address on the enclosed postage free card. There is no obligation whatsoever. *You be the judge*. The important thing is—MAIL THE CARD TODAY.

Members receiving this mailing are misled on at least seven counts.

(1) Using the union's letterhead creates belief that the insurance has the official sanction by labor, which in this and most such union cases is untrue. An arrangement was simply made for the use of the letter and the mailing list, which appears to violate Federal Trade Commission standards for health insurance merchandising:

> No advertisement shall represent directly or by implication that an insurer, or policy or advertisement thereof, has been approved, endorsed, or recommended by an individual, group of individuals, society, association, or other organization, unless such is a fact.[12]

(2) The letter suggests a price discount, though premiums are actually higher than nonunion insurance. This practice is condemned by FTC as follows:

> No advertisement shall represent, directly or indirectly, that prospective policyholders become group or quasi-group members and as such enjoy special rates or underwriting privileges . . . unless such is a fact.[13]

(3) The letter clearly says, "house or hospital confinement not required" for sickness disability, but the policy itself states:

> If such sickness shall totally and continuously disable the insured for one day or more, the company will pay indemnity at the rate of the normal monthly benefit beginning with the first day of medical treatment during disability, but not to

exceed twelve consecutive months for any one sickness, *provided the Insured is continuously confined within doors and treated therein by a licensed doctor of medicine, surgeon, or osteopath other than the insured* [emphasis added].

(4) The term "arbitration privilege" seeks to give the program a union flavor and bring it within labor relations procedures that require American Arbitration Association certification. The policy calls for a three-member board, the enormous cost of which presumably would fall on the union member who requested it. Extensive investigation yields no case in which arbitration was used to negotiate "union" health policies offered in the last ten years.

(5) Illegal in Florida, District of Columbia, Massachusetts, Mississippi, Oregon, Tennessee, Texas, and Wisconsin, the "Waiver of Premium on Strike" provision is unworkable. Members who try to use it usually become frustrated by the red tape: they must write to the company for a special form, get a designated union official to certify that the strike was authorized by the international union, and, in some cases, get the whole thing notarized. This procedure requires more than a month, by which time the member, who has probably received another premium due notice, either pays the premium or drops the policy in disgust.

(6) Representing the policy as having a Guaranteed Renewal Warranty appears in direct conflict with FTC regulations requiring disclosure when advertising renewal provisions. The plan described (Guarantee Trust Form 2021) under the Boilermakers' letterhead has no warranty renewal provision and is not guaranteed renewable due to all the following policy conditions:

> The Company agrees, anything in the policy to the contrary notwithstanding, to renew this policy upon payment before the grace period expires, of the term premium for this policy in effect at the time of renewal, provided: (1) The

Insured is under the age of 65 years at the time of renewal, and (2) The Insured has not retired, and (3) The Insured is a member of the Union Local stated in the copy of the original application attached to this policy, and (4) The Company has not given at least sixty (60) days written notice to the insured that it will not renew all policies issued to members of the aforesaid Union Local, and (5) The issuance of the policy was not procured through false, misleading or omission of statements contained in the copy of the original application attached to this policy, which statements would materially affect either the acceptance of the risk or the hazard assumed by the Company.

(7) The spurious nature of the entire mailing is characterized by use of the term "Union Labor Division" while omitting any reference to the name of the insurance company. Clearly, this offends the FTC rule that:

There shall not be used in an advertisement any trade name, service mark, slogan, symbol, or other device which has the capacity and tendency to mislead or deceive prospective purchasers as to its true identity of the insurer or its relation with public or private institutions.

Using "Union Labor Division" is an apparent attempt to cause union members to associate the program with some familiar agency such as the U.S. Labor Department's Wage and Hour Division, which seems contrary to the FTC rule against representation that any plan of insurance is "approved, endorsed, or recommended by any governmental agency or departments"—unless, of course, such is a fact.[14]

Apparent unfair trade practices and deceptive merchandising in the union labor insurance field appear endless, yet they are ignored by the FTC and state regulatory agencies. The union labor health insurance scheme has been worked for a decade in most states and could hardly go unnoticed by federal and state authorities.

The NALC takes credit for the federal government's failure to act:

> The NALC has worked successfully to frustrate . . . and will continue to work for the frustration of Federal agencies intent on regulation of our companies.[15]

Religious. "Christian" insurance in the Bible Belt, where millions of believers are highly organized—and lately computerized—is big business for general agencies. However, the field is apparently not so lucrative for underwriting companies. Southern Baptists, numbering in the tens of millions, make a substantial market, a potential first recognized by Christian Insurance Associates, Inc., St. Petersburg, Florida, who mass-sell hospital, disability, and Medicare policies to members of Christian organizations.

A full-page message runs continuously in the *Florida Baptist Witness*, the official Florida Baptist Convention paper, with return coupons to " . . . receive completely free information about the plan or plans marked below, that I read about in the *Baptist Witness*." Nothing indicates that it is a paid advertisement, and to the unsuspecting it might well appear as an official Florida Baptist program, particularly in view of the paper's policy of accepting very few advertisements.

Maine Insurance Company, formerly the underwriter for Christian insurance, went into Maine Supreme Court and claimed bankruptcy in February, 1971. Despite financial injury to policyholders who had paid premiums for several months in advance, the court relieved all concerned of further claims liability.[16]

Losing no time, Christian Insurance Associates selected another insurer, Richmond Life Insurance Company. Using their Maine policyholder lists, the company sold these same people some new Christian policies, with full waiting periods. Richmond Life charged full premiums and allowed Christian to withhold full first year front commissions.

Sales paraphernalia at Christian Associates relies strongly on the praying hands featured on advertising matter, such as gold-plated ballpoint pens that are given out free of charge. "When I go into a home flashing the praying hands and making like a front row pew-holder, you just know I've got their attention right off," a writing agent for Christian Associates declared. "But are these people really sincere in their Christian approach?" the agent was asked. "Let's put it this way," was the reply, "they are a damn sight more holy than righteous."[17]

Protective Legislation

Mail solicitation was used extensively a few years ago to sell bootleg insurance, so called since the companies did not bother to qualify their businesses legally in states in which they solicited.[18]

Losing revenue from fees and taxes, the states passed numerous laws, recommended by the National Association of Insurance Commissioners, to control mail order companies. The Unauthorized Insurers Service of Process Act automatically subjects mail order companies to the jurisdiction of state courts in which they solicit by making that state's insurance commissioner an agent for legal process. Hypothetically, a Mack's Creek, Missouri, mail order customer can get judgment against a Philadelphia, Pennsylvania, insurance company after serving process on the Superintendent of Insurance, Jefferson City, Missouri. The customer does not have to go to Pennsylvania to get judgment. But how is the customer to collect? If it followed the normal pattern, the company established no assets in Missouri on which judgment can be levied. The uniform laws for collecting out-of-state judgments are slow and expensive. If a policyholder is hospitalized for two weeks, the average $100 weekly mail order policy supposedly would pay only $100 under the seven-day elimination; if the stay was the average eight days, $14.28 would be paid for each day. Even if the company had assets in Missouri, the expense and delay of a lawsuit would hardly be worthwhile.

Another state effort at legal control requiring all policies, including mail order, to be signed by a licensed resident agent is of little value in collection efforts. This is evidenced by the fact that a retired banker in one state signs policies for seventeen out-of-state mail order companies with which he has no meaningful relationship. He holds none of their assets and has no power to assist policyholders.[19]

The Uniform Reciprocal Licensing Law, a state law with teeth, authorizes insurance commissioners to revoke licenses of domestic insurance companies when they operate illegally in other states. But enforcement of the law requires reciprocity, and not all states have it.

Since they discovered that state laws provide little deterrent, most (but by no means all) companies have found that a solid show of sanctity is a mail order asset; now they boast that they are "licensed by the government of every state of the United States and the District of Columbia."[20] But they continue to dread federal regulation, the only control that could effectively reach them.

According to an NALC publication:

The NALC speaks with knowledge, authority, and respect in its resistance to Federal regulation. It speaks in the corridors of the Capitol, the offices of Senators and Representatives, in the cloakrooms and in the meeting and conference places of the capital city. It speaks as the recognized voice of the younger, smaller companies. And it always speaks in favor of strong state insurance departments. *Through state supervision we have the economic climate for growth* [emphasis added] and the right to develop sound, imaginative insurance products that will meet the mushrooming and changing demands of tomorrow.

One important result of these continuing actions is the splendid relations enjoyed by the NALC with state insurance departments in all sections of the nation.[21]

As a result of the recent organization of Policyholders Protective Association International, one can hope ·that health insurance consumers also will have a voice in the hearing rooms in Washington for the first time in history.

Warning to Mail Order Buyers

Almost without exception, mail order insurance schemes have built-in features to frustrate the collection of claims due to the way that health information is treated. The buyer should bear in mind that *any omission of pertinent health history will be held against policyholders who try to collect.* This abuse is so widespread that the federal government has seen fit to issue the following warning:

> Most insurance sold by mail requires no medical examination; however, the application form requires you to state whether or not you have received medical attention in the past five years and to list any diseases or other physical difficulties you may have had during this period.
>
> Unless you complete this form carefully and accurately, you may find that when you purchase the policy and make a claim, the company will refuse to pay contending that you have a "pre-existing condition" which you failed to mention on the application form.[22]

State laws adopted to protect health insurance policyholders grant companies the right to deny claims up to two years from the date of the application, based on misstatements made by the applicant in the application.[23]

Most mail order solicitations handle health history so loosely that its significance is easily overlooked. For example, Union Fidelity's mail order application has spaces for the applicant's name and as many as five dependents. Further down the application asks, "Has any person named above undergone medical treatment or been hospitalized in the past five years?" Four short lines on a newspaper coupon are provided for the five-year health history of as many as six people.

In its mail order application National Home Life asks just one health question in advertising its Extra Cash Hospitalization Indemnity Plan, Form 10-669. The policy says:

> After 2 years from the date this Policy becomes effective for a covered member hospital confinement commencing thereafter while this policy is in force for such covered member as a result of any condition for which such covered member was medically treated or advised prior to the Effective Date, shall be covered hereunder.

This is simply another way of saying that preexisting conditions are not covered unless the policy has been continuously in force for two years. At claims time the company will, no doubt, try to find such a preexisting condition, which is a highly inexact science even among doctors. (A single trace of urine sugar, slight irregularity in blood pressure, and ordinary indigestion have been used as preexisting conditions by companies denying claims for diabetes, heart attacks, and ulcers, respectively.)

The totality of the massive mail order sales effort is contributing little toward solving the problem of health care financing. In the face of mounting hospital costs the benefits derived from this type of policy are too limited to be of much help. Even more detrimental is the maze of deception that surrounds the entire system.

Since the industry opposes federal regulation and seeks a "creative free enterprise system," the handwriting on the wall clearly says that a voluntary industry-sponsored movement for self-regulation is imperative. But this development is unlikely; competition for the mail order dollar has become so fierce that it will have to be checked by a federal insurance code implemented by strong enforcement machinery.

The following quote, from *Forbes* magazine, enforces this idea:

Like the auto industry, the tire industry, packaging and mutual funds before it, the long nearly sacrosanct insurance business is likely to soon feel the protect the consumer reformist zeal in the U.S. Congress. Certain kinds of companies —mail order outfits, for example—are often run without any regulation at all.[24]

SOURCES

1. Buckley, William F., "Insurance Bug," *Florida Times-Union*. October 28, 1971.
2. Atwood, Albert W., *The Great Stewardship*. New York: Harper Brothers, 1945.
3. Mississippi Insurance Department, *Insurance Commissioner v. Turner Carpenter, et al.* Jackson, Mississippi: 1964. Administrative proceedings in which author was counsel for defendants.
4. Crandell, Melvin G., 916 Beachview Drive, Jekyll Island, Georgia 31520.
5. Interviews with Arthur DeMoss and Harry Dozer. December 9-11, 1970.
6. U.S. Federal Trade Commission, Bureau of Consumer Protection, *Mail Order Insurance, Consumer Bulletin Number 1*. Washington, D.C.: U.S. Government Printing Office, 1971.
7. Stacy, R. A., Grand Secretary, Grand Lodge of New Hampshire, I.O.O.F., general letter to membership. Concord, N.H., undated.
8. Health Insurance Institute, *Source Book of Health Insurance Data*. New York: Health Insurance Institute, 1970.
9. Union Labor Division, Life Assurance Company of Pennsylvania, general letter to members of labor unions, undated.
10. American Income Life Insurance Company, *Annual Report, 1969*. Indianapolis and Waco: 1969.
11. Guarantee Trust Life Insurance Company, *Annual Report, 1969*. Chicago: 1969.
12. U.S. Federal Trade Commission, *Guides for Mail Order Insurance Industry*. Washington: effective July 14, 1964. Guide 9, p. 6.
13. *Ibid.*, Guide 10, p. 6.
14. *Ibid.*, Guide 9.
15. National Association of Life Companies, *Never in a Thousand Years*. Atlanta: 1971.
16. *Wall Street Journal*. February 2, 1971.
17. Williams, Dorothy C., Agent, Christian Insurance Associates, St. Petersburg, Fla., personal interview.
18. Angell, Frank Joseph, *Health Insurance*. New York: Roland Press, 1963.
19. Latham, J.W., Jackson, Mississippi. Personal interview.
20. Bankers Multiple Line Insurance Company, *Magna-Medicare*. Chicago: 1971.
    Globe Life Insurance Company, *Safe-Driver Award*. Chicago: 1971.
21. *Op. Cit.*, National Association of Life Companies, *Never in a Thousand Years*.
22. *Op. Cit.*, Federal Trade Commission, *Mail Order Insurance, Consumer Bulletin Number 1*.

23. Uniform Accident and Sickness Policy Provisions Law, recommended by the National Association of Insurance Commissioners in 1950 and adopted in all states.
24. *Forbes*. December 1, 1966.

If you are tired of being ripped off...

Send a copy of **INSURANCE RIPOFFS AND DIRTY TRICKS: The Sucker's Dilemma** to your federal or state lawmaker to inform him or her that the widespread insurance rackets warrant a complete investigation — and more importantly, **corrective legislation**.

- ✂ - - - -

Please send me ___ copies of **INSURANCE RIPOFFS AND DIRTY TRICKS** at $14.95 each plus $2.00 per copy for shipping and handling. If you are ordering two or more books, shipping and handling is free — you pay just $14.95 each postpaid. California residents please add 6% state sales tax.

Enclosed is my check or money order for $_____, payable to THUMBSDOWNBOOKS.

Mail to THUMBSDOWNBOOKS, P.O. Box ~~89912, San Diego,~~ *261 KIRKLAND,* CA 92138-3912.

PLEASE PRINT CLEARLY, THIS WILL BE YOUR MAILING LABEL.

Name _____

Mailing Address _____

City _____ State _____ Zip _____